100 WA...
Cambridge...
Bedfords...e

compiled by

KATHERINE APPLETON
&
BOB AND CELIA WALLACE

The Crowood Press

First published in 1998 by
The Crowood Press Ltd
Ramsbury
Marlborough
Wiltshire SN8 2HR

British Library Cataloguing-in-Publication Data
A catalogue record for this book is
available from the British Library

ISBN 1 86126 103 9

All maps by Janet Powell

Typeset by Carreg Limited, Ross-on-Wye, Herefordshire

Printed and bound in Great Britain by Biddles Ltd, Guildford and King's Lynn

CONTENTS

Cambridgeshire

34.	Hardwick	$7^1/_2$m	($12^1/_2$km)
35.	Winwick and Old Weston	8m	(13km)
36.	The Riptons	8m	(13km)
37.	… and longer version	$10^1/_2$m	(17km)
38.	St Ives	8m	(13km)
39.	Cheveley	8m	(13km)
40.	Fulbourn	8m	(13km)
41.	Dry Drayton	8m	(13km)
42.	Croxton	8m	(13km)
43.	Whittlesey	8m	(13km)
44.	Kimbolton	8m	(13km)
45.	Spaldwick	8m	(16km)
46.	Croydon	$8^1/_2$m	(13km)
47.	Over	9m	(14km)
48.	Soham	9m	(14km)
49.	Kirtling	9m	(14km)
50.	Meldreth and Melbourn	9m	(14km)
51.	River Nene	9m	(14km)
52.	March	9m	(14km)
53.	Littleport	9m	(14km)
54.	Ely – The Bishops Way	9m	(14km)
55.	Castor	9m	(14km)
56.	… and longer version	11m	(17km)
57.	Sawtry and The Giddings	$9^1/_2$m	(15km)
58.	Rampton	10m	(16km)
59.	Waterbeach and Upware	10m	(16km)
60.	Stilton	10m	(16km)
61.	… and longer version	12m	(19km)
62.	Horseheath	10m	(16km)
63.	Sawston	10m	(16km)
64.	Meldreth and Orwell	10m	(16km)
65.	Barrington	10m	(16km)
66.	The Papworths	10m	(16km)
67.	Bourn	10m	(16km)
68.	Witchford	10m	(16km)
69.	Catworth	10m	(16km)
70.	Sawston	11m	(18km)

Bedfordshire

71.	Stockgrove Country Park	3m	(5km)
72.	… and longer version	7m	(12km)
73.	Harrold and Odell Country Park	4m	(6km)
74.	… and longer version	8m	(12km)
75.	Whipsnade and Studham	4m	(7km)
76.	… and longer version	9m	(14km)
77.	Willington	5m	(7km)
78.	Marston Thrift	5m	(8km)
79.	Houghton House and Maulden	5m	(8km)
80.	The Wootton Walk	5m	(8km)
81.	The Ouse in Bedford	5m	(8km)
82.	Upper Lea Valley	5m	(8km)
83.	Wrest Park	5m	(9km)
84.	Barton Springs	6m	(9km)
85.	Sundon Hills and Sharpenhoe Clappers	6m	(9km)
86.	Totternhoe Knolls	6m	(9km)
87.	Blows Down	6m	(9km)
88.	Stevington Windmill	6m	(10km)
89.	Clophill	7m	(11km)
90.	Old Warden and Northill	7m	(11km)
91.	Everton	7m	(11km)
92.	Salford and Hulcote	7m	(11km)
93.	Hockliffe	7m	(11km)
94.	Ampthill Park and Millbrook	8m	(12km)
95.	Melchbourne	8m	(13km)
96.	The Ouse and Ivel Rivers	8m	(13km)
97.	Elstow	8m	(13km)
98.	River Ouse and Bromham Mill	10m	(16km)
99.	Woburn Park and Heath	11m	(17km)
100.	Turvey	11m	(17km)

PUBLISHER'S NOTE

We very much hope that you enjoy the routes presented in this book, which has been compiled with the aim of allowing you to explore the area in the best possible way - on foot.

We strongly recommend that you take the relevant map for the area, and for this reason we list the appropriate Ordnance Survey maps for each route. Whilst the details and descriptions given for each walk were accurate at time of writing, the countryside is constantly changing, and a map will be essential if, for any reason, you are unable to follow the given route. It is good practice to carry a map and use it so that you are always aware of your exact location.

We cannot be held responsible if some of the details in the route descriptions are found to be inaccurate, but should be grateful if walkers would advise us of any major alterations. Please note that whenever you are walking in the countryside you are on somebody else's land, and we must stress that you should *always* keep to established rights of way, and *never* cross fences, hedges or other boundaries unless there is a clear crossing point.

Remember the country code:

Enjoy the country and respect its life and work
Guard against all risk of fire
Fasten all gates
Keep dogs under close control
Keep to public footpaths across all farmland
Use gates and stiles to cross field boundaries
Leave all livestock, machinery and crops alone
Take your litter home
Help to keep all water clean
Protect wildlife, plants and trees
Make no unnecessary noise

The walks are listed by length - from approximately 1 to 12 miles - but the amount of time taken will depend on the fitness of the walkers and the time spent exploring any points of interest along the way. Nearly all the walks are circular and most offer recommendations for refreshments.

Good walking.

Wisbech

11
29

55/56 Peterborough
51   8   43

60/61   52

                             24

          3   16   53
    30   54
57   31   32   68   20
10   36/37
35   15   23
9

69   45   Huntingdon   38   48
         44   1   26
    21   47   58   59
95   25

    19   66   41   22   4/5   39
         42   34   Cambridge   33   49
                                 2   12
73/74   67   13   40
100   88   96   18   62
    Bedford   91   46   65   63   70   6/7
98   81   77   64   27
80   97   50   17
         90   14
    78
92   94   79   89
         83

99   84
71/72   85
93

86   Luton
    87   82
75/76

Walk 1   **Houghton Meadows**   3m (5km)

Maps: OS Sheets Landranger 153; Pathfinder 960.
A perfect Sunday stroll along the Great Ouse River.
Start: At 282722, the Three Horseshoes Inn, Houghton.

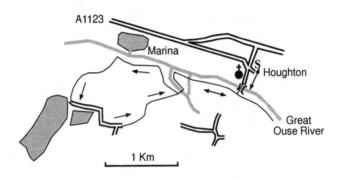

Facing the Three Horseshoes Inn, turn right and walk down the lane signed for
Houghton Mill, passing the statue to Houghton's most famous resident, Potto Brown,
and the church. Follow the public bridleway through the mill and across all parts of
the **Great Ouse River**. Having crossed the lock, turn right and follow the footpath
beside the river, following the signs for the Ouse Valley Way. Continue along the
riverside for about $1^1/_4$ miles, passing weirs and inlets, and then for another 1,000 yards
beside a very slow flowing, smaller part of the river, passing a track and a very pretty
pond to the left.

At the next bridge and a slightly larger track, just beside a horse field, leave the
river, turning left down the track. As a double check, the track should have very high
and thick hedges on both sides. Follow the track around two right-angled bends, one
to the right and then one to the left, to reach a gate. Continue straight ahead, passing

the Fisheries to reach the permitted path immediately ahead. Follow this path, straight on at first, then bearing slightly left and going diagonally to a bridge. You are now back on the Ouse Valley Way and your outward route: retrace your steps beside the river to reach Houghton Lock, Houghton Mill and **Houghton**.

POINTS OF INTEREST:

Houghton Mill – Owned by the National Trust, this is an excellent timber watermill built on an island in the middle of the Great Ouse River. A lot of the 19th-century milling machinery is still intact and is used on milling days, usually Sundays in summer. The mill is open most afternoons throughout the summer.

Great Ouse River – The river's valley provides some of the most interesting and attractive countryside in the county. In such an expanse of dry arable land as Cambridgeshire, the river and its water-filled gravel pits provide a rare and valuable habitat for water species – reeds, rushes and marsh plants; dragonflies and butterflies; and coots, moorhens, swans and other waterfowl. In addition, the river flood meadows provide a permanent grassland habitat rich in mature trees and wild flower species such as cowslips, crosswort and salad burnet.

Houghton – Houghton is a very pretty village, with many thatched houses centred around a small square with a Merchant's Cross at its centre. The village was the winner of the 'Best Kept Village' competition in the Huntingdonshire District in 1987.

St Mary's Church was built mainly in the early 14th century and has a very unusually shaped tower (although there are a number of similar towers in Cambridgeshire) created by the stopping of the strengthening buttresses below the bell openings and then an octagonal continuation. Once the tower also had many ornamental pinnacles around its top, but these were very badly damaged in the hurricane of 1741.

REFRESHMENTS:

The Three Horseshoes Inn, Houghton.

There is a tea-room in Houghton Caravan Park, beside the river.

Maps: OS Sheets Landranger 154; Pathfinder 1004.

The Architecture and Grounds of Cambridge and its Colleges.

Start: At 446593, Cambridge Castle.

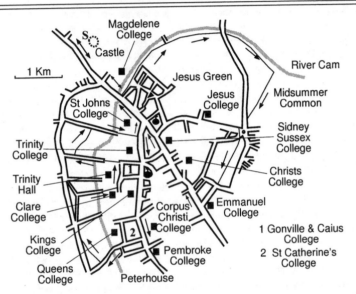

From the castle join the main road and walk downhill, passing **Kettle's Yard**, right, and Magdalene College (originally a Benedictine Hostel, but refounded as a college in 1542. Home to the superb Pepys Library), left. Cross the River Cam and go past St John's College (founded in 1511 by Lady Margaret Beaufort, mother of Henry VII. Haws an imitation Bridge of Sighs over the Cam), right, to reach the **Round Church**, left. Turn right down St John's Street, with some of the finest architecture in the country. Go past Trinity College (founded in 1546 by King Henry VIII. Home of the Wren Library), Gonville and Caius College (founded twice, firstly in 1347 by the priest Gonville and then in 1551 by Dr. Caius, a superb physician and scholar), King's College and Chapel (founded by Henry VI. The chapel is, perhaps, the finest example of English Gothic), right, and **Great St Mary's Church,** left. Continue past St Catherine's College (founded in 1473), right, and Corpus Christi College (which has a reclusive, medieval air. The Saxon tower of the adjoining parish church is 11th-century), left, to the junction with Silver Street. Continue for a further 100 yards to see Pembroke College. Return to the junction and go along Silver Street, passing Queens' College (founded by the Queens Margaret in 1448 and Elizabeth in 1478), right, to reach a signed footpath for The Backs. Go around the building and diagonally across the park to a road. Cross the smaller road and take the path opposite to reach the gate to Clare College (founded in 1338, but rebuilt in the 17th century). Turn into the college grounds and walk through them and the college to reach the street. Turn left, passing the Old School's Building (the University's administrative centre), right, and Trinity Hall (small in comparison to its neighbours, but pleasantly quiet), left, to reach the gateway to Trinity College just before the road bends. Walk through Trinity College and grounds to return to The Backs. Out of the grounds, take the next path on the right into St John's College. Go through the grounds and college to St John's Street. Turn left for 50 yards to the river. Turn right along the near side of the river and walk beside shops and offices, following the path beside Jesus Green and then under the road and beside Midsummer Common. Continue beside the river until opposite the Golden Hawn boathouse. Now take the path on the right across the common and turn left to a roundabout. Go straight across into Christ's Pieces. Walk towards the town and then along a road to reach the main street beside Emmanuel College (founded in 1584 on the site of a Dominican Priory, be sure to see the Wren Chapel). Turn left for 50 yards to visit Emmanuel's College or continue by turning right up St Andrew's Street, into the town centre, passing Christ's College (founded in 1505). At the fork, take the main street, to the left, passing Sidney Sussex College (founded in 1594) to reach Halfords. Turn right down Jesus Lane to Jesus College (founded in place of St Radegund Nunnery which was closed when the nuns were expelled for misbehaviour). Retrace your steps to St Andrew's Street and reverse the outward route to the start.

POINTS OF INTEREST:

Kettle's Yard – Kettle's yard contains an interesting 20th-century art collection complete with paintings, sculptures and furniture.

Round Church – The Church of the Holy Sepulchre, or Round Church, was built in 1130 and is one of only five round churches in England.

Great St Mary's Church – Built in the 15th century in the Perpendicular style of English Gothic the church offers a lovely view over the city from the top of its tower.

REFRESHMENTS:

The walker is spoilt for choice in Cambridge.

Walk 3   **BURY LUG FEN**   4m (6km)

Maps: OS Sheets Landranger 142; Pathfinder 940.
A short walk past the site of a once important abbey.
Start: At 287853, the Market Place, Ramsey.

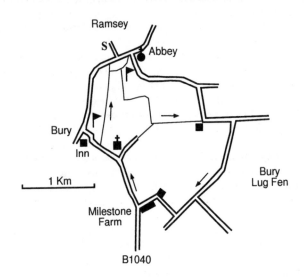

From the Market Place, in the centre of Ramsey, go to the High Street and walk towards **Ramsey Abbey** and **St Mary's Church**, then, soon, turning right along a path signed 'Footpath to Bury Church'. Follow the footpath beside the golf course and through some shaded areas to reach the edge of the fens. Now, do not take the path ahead to the church: instead take the path to your left, follow it as it makes various lefts and rights, though roughly maintaining direction. When the path reaches a track, keep ahead for a short distance, then follow the track around to the right and walk through the fen for about a mile to reach Milestone Farm. If you do get lost, or simply for self assurance, use the buildings and track corners to find your position on the map. Go through Milestone Farm to reach the main road (the B1040). Turn right and follow the path beside the road into Bury to reach the **Church of the Holy Cross**.

You could now take the path through the churchyard, but this will result in retracing your steps towards the end of the walk. So, walk down the road and, just after crossing a bridge, take the signed footpath on the right. Almost immediately, go over another stile on your left so as to walk along the footpath rather than across the golf course. Follow the path into Ramsey, the various path junctions towards the end simply resulting in your arriving on the High Street in different places. Once you are on the High Street the Market Place is easily found.

POINTS OF INTEREST:

Ramsey Abbey – The Abbey was founded by Benedictine monks in 969AD and was one of the most important monastic houses in the county right up to the Dissolution. The abbey was then destroyed, its stones being used to build several of the Cambridge colleges and a number of churches in the area. The original Chapel House remained, however. It has had numerous alterations and additions so is rather a mix of styles. It is currently used as a Grammar School. Also on the site is the Gatehouse, a very fine piece of architecture.

St Mary's Church, Ramsey – This very large church was built in 1858 and has some excellent stained-glass windows.

Church of the Holy Cross, Bury – This large, well-kept church is thought to have been built around the 13th century, although precise dates for certain parts have proved rather puzzling.

REFRESHMENTS:

The White Lion, Bury.
There are numerous opportunities in Ramsey.

LODE

4m (6km)
or $10^1/_2$m (17km)

Maps: OS Sheets Landranger 154; Pathfinder 982.
Picturesque fenland countryside and villages.
Start: At 534627, the Post Office, High Street, Lode.

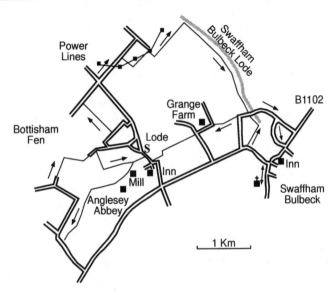

From the Post Office, cross the road and follow the path signed for Quy Fen and the Baptist Chapel. Follow the path past the chapel and some allotments, and then maintain direction (despite any confusing path arrows) to reach **Lode Watermill**. Walk beside the mill, cross a small drain and then follow the Harcamlow Way beside the river, behind **Anglesey Abbey**. Follow the Way to a road and turn right. Walk around the right bend, then, at the left bend, go ahead along a track, following it to the left to reach a fork. Take the right-hand branch and, at its end, enter a field and bear right along a path. Follow the path through fields, across a bridge and around a field edge to reach a wide grassy track. Walk down the track.

The short walk takes the first signed footpath on the right. Follow the path back to the watermill, then retrace your steps back to the start.

The longer walk takes the first signed footpath on the left. Follow this track and then a path around and across fields to reach another track. Turn right and walk to a road. Cross the road slightly left and walk down a track to reach a signed path just after having passed under the electricity lines. Go ahead along the path, then bear left to reach a track. Turn right to the end of the track. Cross a bridge and follow the edge of the field ahead. At the far end of the field, keep ahead into the next field, and then turn left immediately to follow a path around the edges of several fields and a small wood to reach the embankment of **Swaffham Bulbeck Lode**. Turn right and follow the lode to reach a road at the second bridge. Turn left, and then take the next road on the right, following it to the main road (the B1102). Turn right and walk to the centre of the village. At the sharp right-hand corner, follow the minor road ahead for 500 yards to visit **St Mary's Church**. The walk follows the main road around the sharp right corner to reach a signed path on the right. Follow the path across a field and then turn left along a track beside trees to reach the road bridge passed earlier. Turn left along the road to the left-hand corner. Here go slightly right, then follow the signed path to the left across a field to reach the corner of Grange Farm. Walk along the track, then take the signed tarmac path slightly to your left. At a path junction, take the path to the left to reach a road. Turn right and walk around the corner to reach **St James' Church** and the Post Office.

POINTS OF INTEREST:

St James's Church, Lode – Built in 1853 this relatively recent and very inconspicuous church has a bellcote and an unusual large wooden porch.

Lode Watermill – The mill still has all its machinery intact and grinds corn on the first Sunday of every month. Admission to the mill is free.

Anglesey Abbey and Gardens, Lode – The Abbey, a National Trust property, is a beautiful manor house surrounded by lovely grounds beside the river. There are magnificent flower displays, most notably in the spring (hyacinths) and in the summer (dahlias). The house and gardens are open on most days throughout the summer.

Swaffham Bulbeck Lode – This man-made channel of water in an otherwise rather dry landscape has become a habitat for a wide variety of wildlife.

St Mary's Church, Swaffham Bulbeck – The interior of this 14th-century church is interesting due to the quality of the wood carvings. Note, especially, the benches.

REFRESHMENTS:

The Black Horse, Swaffham Bulbeck.

The Camps   4m (7km)
or 9m (15km)

Maps: OS Sheets Landranger 154; Pathfinder 1028.
Two fine walks through typical Cambridgeshire countryside.
Start: At 633432, the centre of Castle Camps.

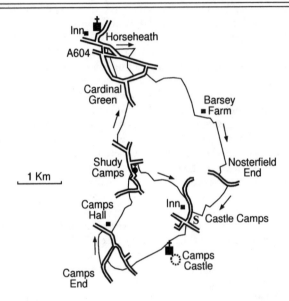

Go down Park Lane, then take the footpath ahead across a field. Turn right and follow the well-trodden path to **All Saints' Church** and **Camps Castle**. Continue through the graveyard and then as before to reach a road. Turn right, but soon take the path on the left, going diagonally across a field to a stile in the corner. Cross and maintain direction to a road. Here turn left into Camps End. At the corner, take the lane on the right, following it around a right-hand bend (not over the stile). Now follow the field edges, keeping the hedges to your left, to reach a road at Camps Hall. Turn right, then, at the corner, take the path on the left. Follow this path for a mile, then, where it forks, take the left branch to reach a road. Cross and walk up the obvious path through a field to reach Shudy Camps (the last part of the path being through a field to avoid a corner of the road). Turn left to **St Mary's Church**.

The shorter walk takes the road on the right (to Nosterfield End) after the church. After about 200 yards, take the signed path on the right, following it through gardens and along field edges to reach the road in Castle Camps. Turn right to regain the start.

The longer walk continues along the road past the church and takes the first road on the left, to Bartlow. After about 500 yards, beyond the buildings, take the path on the right, following it around two field edges. Now, where you have a choice (of ahead or left) turn left and follow a signed path to a road. Turn left into Cardinal's Green. At the road junction, turn left to reach a signed path on the right, just before a bend in the road. Follow the path, then take the left fork to reach the main road (the A604). Cross, with care, and follow the road opposite but slightly to the right. At the end, turn left into the centre of Horseheath. **All Saints' Church** is 200 yards along the road to West Wickham, the inn is on the road to Linton and Cambridge. Walk towards Haverhill, then take the path off the sliproad to your left. Follow it to a hedge and turn right to the road. Cross, with care, and take the path to Cardinals Green. At the road, turn left to the corner and take the signed footpath to the right. Take the right-hand path diagonally across a field, then beside trees and diagonally across another field to a stream. Follow the stream for about $^1/_2$ mile, keeping to its left, then, beyond a small clump of trees, take the track on the left to Barsey Farm. Turn right along the bridleway at the field edge, in front of the house, following it for just over a mile to a road at Nosterfield End. Turn left for about 500 yards, then take the path on the right immediately before a house. Follow this path to the road in Castle Camps. (At a small clump of scrub, keep to the right and follow the dyke as it goes right, then left). Turn left to the village centre.

POINTS OF INTEREST:
All Saints' Church, Castle Camps – This flint and stone church has been so much restored that its date is not definite.
Camps Castle – This was a Norman motte and bailey castle built in William I's reign by Aubrey de Vere.
St Mary's Church, Shudy Camps – Apart from the southern chancel doorway, which is 13th-century, the church is entirely in Perpendicular style. It houses many interesting paintings and sculptures.
All Saints' Church, Horseheath – Mainly Decorated English Gothic, but with a nave in Perpendicular style, the height, and the light, make the interior very pleasant.

REFRESHMENTS:
The Camps Castle, Castle Camps.
The Cock, Castle Camps.
The Old Red Lion, Horseheath.

Walk 8   **PETERBOROUGH**   4m (7km)

Maps: OS Sheets Landranger 142; Pathfinder 918.

The beauty of art and nature.

Start: At 193987, Cathedral Square, Peterborough.

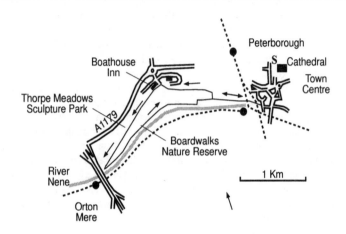

From the Cathedral Square, with your back to the **Cathedral**, facing the **Market Place**, turn left down Bridgate. Walk through the town, passing the Town Hall, a very grand building, on your left. Cross the dual carriageway, with care, and continue to the sign for Railworld, on the right. Go under the arch and, at the end of the road (on reaching Asda), turn left to reach the **River Nene**. Keeping on this side of the river, turn right along the riverside path, following this tarmac path under the **Iron Bridge** and the railway bridge. Go past **Railworld**, on the other side of the river keeping to the tarmaced path, then, at the end of the path, cross the bridge and follow the path beside the Boathouse Inn, keeping the inn to your right. Continue along the path through **Thorpe Meadows Sculpture Park**. At the end of the Park, continue along the path, then, just before going under the road bridge, turn left along the well-trodden path beside the river, going through the **Boardwalks Local Nature Reserve**. Follow the path past a red footbridge to arrive back on the tarmac path. Turn right and retrace your steps back into Peterborough.

POINTS OF INTEREST:

Peterborough Cathedral – The Cathedral is built on what has been a site of worship for almost 2000 years. The first church here was built in 665AD, but this was destroyed during a raid. A Benedictine Abbey was built in 972, but this, too, was destroyed, though this time accidentally by fire. The present building was constructed in 1118 and made a Cathedral by King Henry VIII. The Cathedral is one of the finest Norman buildings in the country and includes a very impressive West Front. The interior is also well worth exploring. It has a beautifully painted ceiling and houses the tomb of Katharine of Aragon.

Market Place – Situated in the centre of the town, beside the Cathedral, the medieval Market Place, and Cathedral Square, are very beautiful.

River Nene – As with the other rivers running through the dry and flat countryside of Cambridgeshire, the Nene provides a valuable habitat for various water species, including reeds, rushes and waterlilies, dragonflies and butterflies and numerous waterbirds including coots, moorhens, swans, geese and the odd kingfisher.

Iron Bridge – This historic bridge was originally part of the Great Northern Railway. Designed by Lewis Cubbitt and built in 1850, it is thought to be one of the few original bridges of its type in Britain. Apart from a few minor repairs in the early 1900s it is as built and possibly the only one in the country still in use.

Railworld – An impressive and comprehensive rail museum, Railworld provides plenty of information and enjoyment on the numerous aspects of rail travel, ranging from pioneering locomotives, local history and a working steam railway, right up to modern rail networks and travel.

Thorpe Meadows Sculpture Park – Situated in a beautiful spot beside the River Nene, the Sculpture Park is a fantastic mix of the beauty of nature and modern art. There are numerous sculptures, all by local artists. The works include Peterborough Arch, Festival Boat, Lagoon, Helios II, Odd Oaks, Endless Omen, Boundaries, and Second Entrance.

Boardwalks Local Nature Reserve – Left to run wild, but now managed, this small area beside the river provides a vital habitat for numerous plant and animal species, both dry and wetland species, including, at the right time of year, vast numbers of dragonflies, damselflies and other insects, and a wide variety of birds.

REFRESHMENTS:

The Boathouse Inn, at the entrance to the Thorpe Meadows Sculpture Park. There are also numerous opportunities in Peterborough.

Walk 9   **ALCONBURY AND BUCKWORTH**   5m (8km)

Maps: OS Sheets Landranger 142; Pathfinder 959.

A delightful walk through typical fenland country.

Start: At 186761, the village pump, Alconbury.

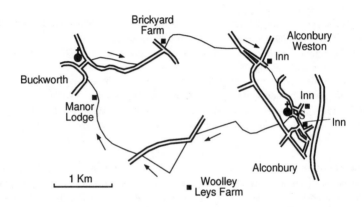

Walk up Church Way, towards the church, to reach a signed path on the left about half-way to the church. Follow this path across Alconbury Brook to reach a road. Turn right, soon reaching a field entrance on the left. Follow a path diagonally across the field to reach a hedge end (as an alternative you may wish to walk around the field edge to the right). Cross the next field along the same diagonal path and, at the bottom, cross a stile and follow the path beyond along the field edge to a road. Turn left as far as the right-hand corner. From here you need to reach the bridleway the other side of the trees from the road. The current entrance is unofficial and not obvious, but can be found by entering the field on the left just before the corner and following its edge to the right to reach a small plank bridge. Cross to join the bridleway next to the trees.

Follow the bridleway to reach a track at the top, then turn right and follow the track to a road. Cross and turn slightly left to follow the obvious bridleway up the hill. Maintain direction at the top, following the track to Manor Lodge Farm. On reaching the farm buildings, keep to the right and head directly across a field towards the end corner of the houses at Buckworth. At the road, maintain direction past the houses, and then turn right to reach **All Saints' Church**.

Continue to the end of the road and turn right. Now, almost immediately, turn left along a signed bridleway. Walk around the edge of a farm, then go straight ahead, through a field, heading eastwards along the obvious path to reach a road. Turn left and follow the road to a T-junction. Cross and take the public bridleway opposite through Brickyard Farm/Stables/Riding School. Follow the bridleway along the edge of one field then, at the next, turn right and follow a footpath along its right-hand side. Maintain direction, as signed, through several fields into Alconbury Weston. Cross Alconbury Brook and turn right to walk into the centre of the village.

At the central crossroads, take the road beside the inn and, at its end, follow the obvious tarmac footpath to Alconbury. On reaching **Alconbury Church**, take the path through the graveyard and, at the other side, walk down Church Way to return to the start.

POINTS OF INTEREST:

St Peter and St Paul's Church, Alconbury – The church was built in the 13th century in Early English style, with a steeple and chancel of notably high quality. In the case of the chancel, the high quality can be seen both inside and out.

All Saints' Church, Buckworth – The church has a splendid late 13th-century steeple. The rest of the church is thought to be slightly earlier, although dates are not definite. The oldest part of the church are the eastern angles of the nave, which are Norman.

REFRESHMENTS:

The White Hart, Alconbury Weston.
The Crown, Alconbury.
The Manor House Hotel, Alconbury.

Walk 10   SAWTRY AND ALCONBURY   5m (8km)

Maps: OS Landranger 142; Pathfinder 939 and 959.
A delightful linear walk through fenland, returning by bus.
Start: At 167837, the parade of shops, Sawtry.

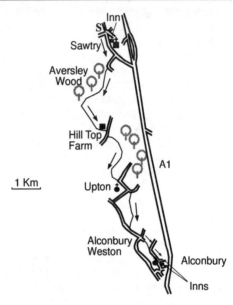

Facing away from the shops, turn right and walk down the main road for about 1,000 yards, passing **All Saints' Church** to your left, to reach St Judith's Lane, on the right. Walk down this to reach a right-angled bend to the left. Here, keep straight on, through a car park, to reach a footpath, following it past some allotments and through fields, crossing several stiles. Walk beside **Aversley Wood**, to the right, to reach its far corner. Turn left along a byway, following it down to a road at Hilltop Farm. Turn right, then left along a track, following it along a field edge. When the track veers left to woodland, go straight on along a grassy track. Follow this bridleway around a wiggle to the left to join a gravel track. Almost immediately, turn right down another track, following it to a hedge. There, turn left along a bridleway to reach a lane in Upton. Follow the lane to **Upton Church** and continue down the road from the church, going past a pond to reach a lane, on the right, signed as a public footpath.

Walk to the end of this lane, then follow a signed path through a garden. Continue straight across two fields, heading for Alconbury Church. In the next field, head for the right-hand corner of the two barns to the right. Cross a field to its track entrance, then cross the next field heading towards the left-hand corner of a barn. Walk past the barn and follow the footpath through the undergrowth to reach the main road through Alconbury Weston. Turn left and walk into the centre of the village. At the central crossroads, take the road beside the inn and, at its end, follow the obvious tarmac footpath into Alconbury. On reaching the church, take the path through the graveyard and, at the other side, walk down Church Way to the village centre and maintain direction down the road to reach the village green.

The return to Sawtry is by bus. The bus leaves the Alconbury Village Green, approximately once every hour from Monday to Saturday except in the middle of the day when it leaves once every two hours. On Sundays there are buses every four hours.

POINTS OF INTEREST:

All Saints' Church, Sawtry – Built in 1880 by Sir A Blomfield, the church has no tower or steeple, but a very steep and detailed bellcote. It houses a number of interesting artefacts including outstandingly good brasses and pieces from Sawtry Abbey.

Aversley Wood – The wood is currently owned by the Woodland Trust and as such is a conservation area providing a vital and well-maintained habitat for local wildlife, including many species of plants and flowers; several species of bird including game birds; and a variety of mammals including hares, deer and weasels.

St Margaret's Church, Upton – This small church has a short broach spire thought to date from Norman times, that is before the mid-13th century.

REFRESHMENTS:

The Bell Inn, Sawtry.
The White Hart, Alconbury Weston.
The Crown Inn, Alconbury.
The Manor House Hotel, Alconbury.

Walk 11   DEEPING ST JAMES   5m (8km)

Maps: OS Sheets Landranger 142; Pathfinder 897.

A pleasant short walk through excellent fenland.

Start: At 148096, the Crown and Anchor Inn, Deeping St James.

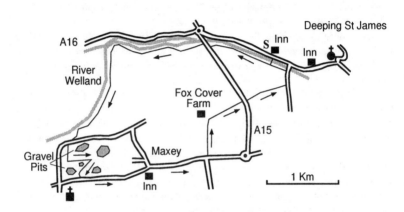

From the inn, cross the road and the footbridge straight ahead, over the weirs and sluices of the **River Welland**. Turn right along the signed riverside path, walking upstream to reach the main road (the A15). Cross, with care, and turn right towards Market Deeping, but soon, turn left along a footpath starting at the beginning of the Birch Bridge Wall, going over a stile. Follow the edge of a field around to the right to rejoin the river. Now walk along the riverbank, with the road (and traffic) just beyond the hedge. At the obvious river junction, continue along the same riverbank, now heading away from the road.

Continue along the riverbank for almost 2 miles, then turn left at a dyke bordered by willow trees. A footpath arrow on a post will appear after about 50 yards, just as a check. Follow the path around the edge of a field, keeping to the right to reach a footbridge in the far corner. Cross on to a lane and turn right. After about 20 yards, cross the first footbridge on the left. The bridge is signed as a footpath. Follow the path around to the left, between fields, passing several lakes on the left (**Maxey Gravel Pits**). At a lane, turn left and maintain direction to reach a path on the right, just before the gateposts (and the point where the lane turns into a road). Follow the path between lakes to reach a road. Here, turn right for about 500 yards to visit **St Peter's Church, Maxey**. The walk turns left, following the road past several lovely thatched cottages and the Blue Bell Inn. Continue, reaching a road to the right for Etton. Do not turn right along this road: instead, turn left along a farm track, following it around to the right and then through several fields (as indicated by the footpath arrows), turning left, then right across a dyke and finally going along the edge of a field to reach the main road (the A15). Cross, with care, and follow the track ahead. At the next road (Deeping St James Road) turn left and, after about 200 yards, turn left again, just before the bridge, to go along the riverside footpath. Now reverse the first few steps of the route back to the start.

POINTS OF INTEREST:

St Peter's Church, Maxey – This broad church with a broad spire dates from the 12th century and is mainly Norman, though various Perpendicular and Decorated features can also be seen.

River Welland and Maxey Gravel Pits – The River Welland, forming the northern boundary of Cambridgeshire, and the Maxey Gravel Pits, created by gravel extraction and subsequently filled with water, both provide valuable wetland habitats for a variety of wildlife including plants such as reeds, rushes and water lilies, and waterbirds such as coots, moorhens and swans.

REFRESHMENTS:

The Crown and Anchor, Deeping St James.
The Blue Bell Inn, Maxey.

Walk 12   **BRINKLEY**   5m (8km)

Maps: OS Sheets Landranger 154; Pathfinder 1005.

A fine walk through typical countryside, visiting some interesting churches.

Start: At 629548, St Mary's Church, Brinkley.

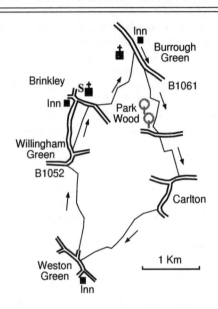

From St **Mary's Church**, Brinkley, go eastwards along the road, then take the path on the left, signed for Burrough Green. Follow the path for about $^1/_2$ mile to reach a lane in Burrough Green. Turn left to visit **St Augustine's Church** then retrace your steps and continue along the lane to reach the main road (the B1061). Turn right, with care, for about 500 yards to reach a footpath, on the right, signed for Carlton. Follow this path straight across a field and then around the left-hand side of Park Wood. At the end of the wood turn left (as waymarked) to reach a road. Cross and continue along the path opposite to reach a road at Carlton.

Turn right and follow the road to a Y-junction. Take the left-hand road, following it for about 500 yards, then, at a left bend, bear right along a narrow lane, passing **St Peter's Church**. At the end of the lane, take the path going diagonally across a field. Cross a bridge and walk beside a field to reach a track. Cross the track and maintain direction across another field. Cross a bridge and another field to its corner, then follow the edges of several fields to reach a road in Weston Green.

Turn right for about 200 yards, then turn right along a lane (this is the first lane on the right). Follow the lane to its end and then follow the bridleway ahead. Nearing Willingham Green, turn left along a public byway to reach a road (the B1052). Turn right, with care, for about 200 yards, passing a road on the left, then take the signed path for Brinkley on the right, through the fenced corner. Follow the path for about $^1/_2$ mile, to reach the road in Brinkley, opposite the church.

POINTS OF INTEREST:

St Mary's Church, Brinkley – This church shows an excellent mix of Perpendicular and Victorian architecture. The tower is Perpendicular. The chancel is Victorian, yet the east window is undoubtedly Perpendicular. The back porch is also Perpendicular and is in fact rather a rare example of the type in Cambridgeshire.

St Augustine's Church, Burrough Green – Though mainly built in the 14th century, the church shows a very interesting variety and mixture of architectural styles. It houses a number of interesting and unusual monuments, mainly of knights and their ladies.

St Peter's Church, Carlton – This small church dates from the 13th and 14th centuries and is an excellent example of the architecture of the period as it has never been added to, restored or rebuilt.

REFRESHMENTS:

The Red Lion, Brinkley.
The Bull, Burrough Green.
The Fox and Hounds, Weston Green.

Walk 13   **GRANTCHESTER**   5m (8km)

Maps: OS Sheets Landranger 154; Pathfinder 1004.

A beautiful Sunday stroll from Cambridge.

Start: At 448584, the Tourist Information Office, Cambridge.

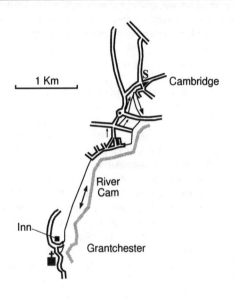

From the Tourist Information Office in the centre of Cambridge, turn right and walk on to Kings Parade. Turn left and follow the street until you are standing in front of Pembroke College. Now turn right into Mill Lane. Walk to the end of the street and cross the **River Cam**. Now take the path to your left, walking beside the river, and crossing parks, roads and bridges to reach a collection of houses. Here, turn right, following the river through **Paradise Nature Reserve**.

Follow the path through the Reserve, then, at the end, turn right along the road ahead (as signed for Grantchester). At the end of the road, maintain direction to join a lovely tarmac path: follow this path all the way to Grantchester.

On arriving in Grantchester, turn right to reach the village centre, the **Church of St Andrew and St Mary** and the village inns. To return to the homeward path, either take the small lane between the Red Lion and Green Man Inns, or turn left down to the river and then return to the path by turning left and climbing back up the hill to reach the path at the top. Turning right at the river will take to the Orchard Tea Rooms.

Unfortunately, to return to Cambridge you will need to retrace your steps along this path – but the path offers very easy walking, and the view of Cambridge on the return is lovely. Alternative meandering, riverside paths can be taken at the end of the walk.

POINTS OF INTEREST:

River Cam – The Cam, a tributary of the Great Ouse River, is one of the most beautiful and atmospheric of rivers in England. Meandering through the dry and flat farmland of the fens, the river provides a striking contrast both in scenery and in its wildlife, this ranging from reeds and water-lilies, to pondskaters and kingfishers. Due to its popularity the river is also well-endowed with delightful riverside inns and teashops, and provides a variety of excellent boating opportunities.

Paradise Nature Reserve – This area of woodland, scrub and undergrowth beside the river is very rich in wildlife. Plant species include reeds, rushes and bramble; there are numerous species of insect; and birds include woodpeckers, coots and moorhens.

The Church of St Andrew and St Mary, Grantchester – The church, which has a notably fine chancel, was built in 1877, though remains of an earlier Norman church do exist and, in places, have been incorporated into the present building.

REFRESHMENTS:

The Red Lion, Grantchester.
The Green Man, Grantchester.
The Orchard Tearooms, Grantchester.
Cambridge has something for all tastes and budgets.

Walk 14   GREAT CHISHILL   5m (8km)

Maps: OS Sheets Landranger 154; Pathfinder 1027 and 1050.
A walk through typical Cambridgeshire countryside, including some lovely views.
Start: At 422389, St Swithun's Church, Great Chishill.

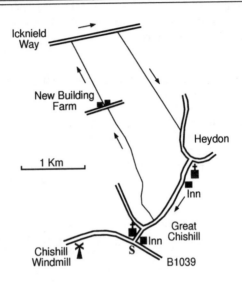

From **St Swithun's Church** in Great Chishill, take the road to Heydon, following it for about 400 yards, then turning right along a footpath to the left, under the evergreens. Follow this lovely, and well-used, path for about 2 miles to reach the **Icknield Way**, making sure you do not turn off the path by going left near the start. Turn right along the Icknield Way, following this grassy track for almost a mile to reach the Harcamlow Way, on your right, opposite a small clump of trees. Take this path, following it for just over a mile to reach a road. Turn right and walk into Heydon. At **Holy Trinity Church**, and the three-way road junction, take the road for Great Chishill, following it for about a mile to return to the start. To reach the Windmill, turn right along the B1039 for about $^3/_4$ mile.

POINTS OF INTEREST:
St Swithun's Church, Great Chishill – The church is built of flint, and seems to have features which date from almost every century from the 12th onwards. Interestingly, although the church does not look to have been added to or rebuilt, it is not completely symmetrical.

Icknield Way – This famous prehistoric highway links Salisbury Plain, in Dorset, to the Wash, in Norfolk.

Holy Trinity Church, Heydon – The church was hit by a bomb in 1940, so little remains apart from the chancel and Perpendicular arcades.

Chishill Windmill – This lovely post mill is an interesting example of rural engineering. It was built in 1819 with timbers from a previous mill of 1726. The mill operated until 1951 and was restored in 1966. It is now a scheduled historic monument and is open to the public from April to October.

REFRESHMENTS:
The Pheasant, Great Chishill.
The King William IV, Heydon.

Walk 15   **ABBOTS RIPTON AND WOODWALTON** $5^1/_2$m (9km)
Maps: OS Sheets Landranger 142; Pathfinder 960 and 940.
Typical fenland villages and countryside.
Start: At 231780, St Andrew's Church, Abbots Ripton.

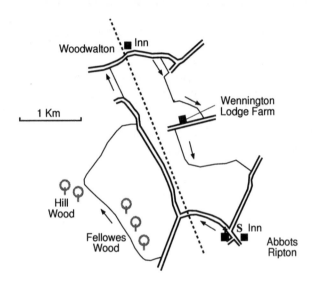

From **St Andrew's Church**, walk out of Abbots Ripton, heading northwards along
the road for about 1,000 yards to reach, just after the railway, a road on the left signed
for the Clay Lane Industrial Area. Take this road, following it to a fork, with a footpath
sign on the right. Take the right-hand track, following it beside the **wood** and around
a corner. Continue along the path ahead for $1^1/_4$ miles to reach a corner of the wood
and a three-way path junction. Take the track heading straight across the fields ahead
to reach a road. Turn left for about 500 yards to reach a public bridleway on the right.
Follow the bridleway downhill, with a lovely view towards Peterborough, to reach a
road. Turn right, walk underneath the railway and into the village of Woodwalton.

Follow the road through the village and then, after rounding a slight left-hand bend, take the signed footpath to the right. Follow the footpath, staying to the right of a fence and then, at the top of the field, cross the middle of the next field to reach a track at the top of the hill. Turn right along the track, following it around a corner and down to a small brook. Turn left along the footpath beside the brook to reach a road. Turn right to reach track on the left, just after Wennington Lodge Farm. Follow the track southwards, then eastwards for approximately $1^1/_4$ miles to reach a road. Turn right and walk back into Abbots Ripton. At the main road, turn left, soon reaching the church.

POINTS OF INTEREST:

St Andrew's Church, Abbots Ripton – This typical country village church, with a tower and graveyard, was founded in 970AD, but then rebuilt in 1242AD though various parts of the building are of different materials suggesting later work as well.

Fellowes Wood and Hill Wood – Both these woods are currently designated as conservation areas and provide vital habitats for local wildlife, typically game birds (peasants, partridges and grouse) and small mammals (mice, voles, rabbits and hares). Neither wood can be entered but the wildlife can be seen overspilling on to the path.

REFRESHMENTS:
The Three Horseshoes, Abbots Ripton.
The Elephant and Castle, Woodwalton.

Walk 16   **CHATTERIS** $5^1/_2$m (9km)

Maps: OS Sheets Landranger 142; Pathfinder 940 and 941.

A fine walk from a typical fenland town.

Start: At 394861, St Peter and St Paul's Church, Chatteris.

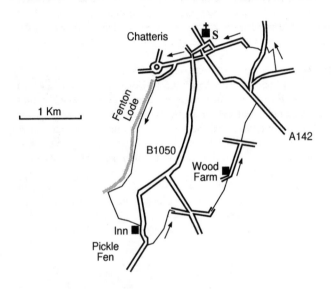

From **St Peter and St Paul's Church** in the centre of Chatteris, walk westwards, following signs for the A141 to Huntingdon. Just before the roundabout, turn left down Huntingdon Road. Virtually at its end the road crosses **Fenton Lode** (the Twenty Foot Drain). Take either of the footpaths beside the lode. Walk along the lode for just over a mile to reach an arched concrete bridge. You need now to be on the eastern side of the lode (ie. if you crossed the lode at the beginning you now need to cross back). Walk along the public byway away from the lode, crossing the fen to reach the main road (the B1050).

Turn right, with care, and walk approximately 500 yards, passing the inn. Just around a right-hand bend, take a track on the left, beside a horse's field, signed as a permitted path. Follow the track around to the left, then follow the path ahead until you can go ahead no longer. Here, turn right and follow a track to a road. Cross and maintain direction along a public byway. This track is a little overgrown initially, soon turns into a sandy track, and then becomes overgrown again (although slightly less so). Follow the track for $1^1/_2$ miles to reach the main road (the A142). Turn left, with care, and follow the road to reach a signed track on the right. Follow the track past fields and around a left-hand bend. When the track ends, continue straight on along the edge of a field and then over a bridge and around to the left. Continue towards the road until a path branches off into a small, tree-lined field: take this path to reach the main road. Cross, with care, and continue along the path opposite. Go diagonally across a playing field, then take the first road on the right, following it to its end. Take the footpath going left and, at its end, maintain direction along a street for 500 yards or so to reach the main road and the centre of Chatteris. The church is just to your right.

POINTS OF INTEREST:

St Peter and St Paul's Church, Chatteris – This high and spacious church, with a fine tower, dates from the 14th century and has a rather unusual nave due to the absence of any stained glass windows and the use of chairs as opposed to pews. It stands on the site of Chatteris Abbey built in 980AD but destroyed in 1000 by rampaging Danes. There was an earlier church on the site, but this unfortunately burnt to the ground in 1310.

Fenton Lode – Although a man-made feature, this wide channel of water in an otherwise rather dry landscape has become a natural habitat for a wide variety of water species including many reeds, rushes and marsh plants, a number a species of insect, most notably dragonflies and butterflies, and a variety of birds including coots, moorhens and swans. The embankments are also home to a great variety and abundance of wild flowers.

REFRESHMENTS:

The Crafty Fox, Pickle Fen.
There is a wide variety of choice in Chatteris.

Walk 17   **FOWLMERE**   6m (10km)

Maps: OS Sheets Landranger 154; Pathfinder 1026 and 1027.

An excellent walk, including a fine Nature Reserve.

Start: At 421458, the three-way junction in the centre of Fowlmere.

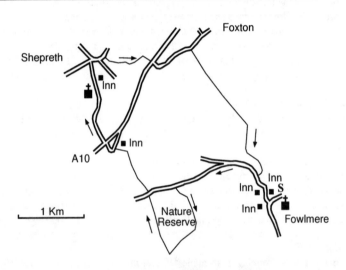

From the central road junction, walk northwards along the road to Shepreth and after almost a mile turn left. At the RSPB sign, turn left and follow the track down to the **Fowlmere Nature Reserve**. Go through a gate and turn left long a path, following it around the outside of the Reserve, passing a small pond and a wooden hut. Now turn right, with the path, and then, as the path continues around to the right, cross the stile on your left, leaving the reserve. Follow the track beyond the stile to reach a road. (If you are walking with a dog you will not be able to walk through the Reserve. Instead, go through the gate and walk beside the Reserve to reach the road. Turn left to rejoin the walk. All dogs should be kept on a very close lead or, preferably, left at home.)

Turn right, but soon turn left along a path for Shepreth. Follow this beautiful path beside a stream finishing along a track which bends around to the left to reach a road. Turn left, then right down Frogs End to reach the A10. Cross, with care, and follow the road opposite into Shepreth, passing **All Saints' Church** and continuing for a further $^1/_2$ mile to reach the village centre.

Turn right, then right again. Continue along the next road on the left, Angle Lane, then turn right, along a lane signed to Foxton. At the end of the lane, take the path signed for Foxton. Go through a gate and past empty ground to reach a path on the left just before a white gate. Follow this path along the edge of a field, then around to the left, past a lake and through woodland. At the other side of the woodland, turn right to reach the main road (the A10). Cross, with care, and take the road opposite towards Foxton. Follow the road for almost $^1/_2$ mile to reach Caxton Lane on the right. Follow this and the track beyond for about a mile, and follow the obvious path through three fields and around the corner beside houses to reach a road. Turn left to return to the start in **Fowlmere**.

POINTS OF INTEREST:

Fowlmere Nature Reserve – This small area of wetland and marshland is a haven for many wetland plant and animal species, particularly birds. Coots, moorhens and swans can often be seen, but the Reserve also attracts various migratory species including geese and terns.

All Saints' Church, Shepreth – Originally built in the Norman era, the church still has that appearance, despite having been restored and renovated in the 17th, 18th and 19th centuries.

Shepreth was the winner of the 'Best Kept Village in Cambridgeshire' Award in 1985.

Fowlmere – St Mary's Church is Norman, but was much restored in 1869 in the Decorated English Gothic style of the 14th century. The church has some very fine battlements, an unusual spike on the top of its tower and a beautiful frieze of vine tendrils and bellflowers on the front of the north transept.

REFRESHMENTS:

The Queen's Head, Fowlmere.
The Black Horse, Fowlmere.
The Chequers Inn, Fowlmere.
The Green Man, Shepreth.
The Plough, Shepreth.

Walk 18   THE EVERSDENS   6m (10km)

Maps: OS Sheets Landranger 154; Pathfinder 1003.

Fine villages and excellent views.

Start: At 366533, the Church of St Mary the Virgin, Great Eversden.

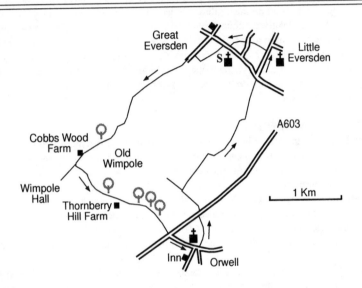

Take the grassy track running along the right-hand side of the **Church of St Mary the Virgin**, following it for about 500 yards to reach a lane. Turn left, following the lane as it turns into a track: continue to reach some buildings. Continue along the signed track (almost the same direction), following it around the edge of a field, and then around a right-angled bend to the right at the top. Continue along the track, going around the wood and down through **Cobbs Wood Farm**, heading towards Old Wimpole and **Wimpole Hall**. After passing the farm buildings, on your right, you will reach two houses on your left. Here, turn left along a footpath, following it beside the river for about 500 yards. Now, after reaching the corner of a wood and crossing a stile, turn left and walk diagonally across a field to a gate. Go through and diagonally straight across the field beyond to the gate in the far corner. Go through and follow the path ahead around the edge of the woods to reach the A603.

Cross, with care, and take the road opposite to reach Orwell and **St Andrew's Church**. Take the path beside the church, going up steps and diagonally across a field, passing a massive pit and then bearing left to reach the main road again. Cross, again with care, and turn right, soon reaching a lane on your left. Follow this to a house, on the left, then take the path on the right along the edge of a field to reach the top of the hill. Turn right along The Mare Way, then take the signed bridleway on the left, following this grassy track into Little Eversden, taking care towards the end to branch left so as not to reach the A603 again. On reaching the road at the end of the track, cross and head up the High Street, Little Eversden, opposite. After about 500 yards you will reach a path for Great Eversden on your left. The walk takes this, but to visit **St Helen's Church** continue along the High Street for a further 100 yards, and then turn right. The path to Great Eversden is obvious, and reaches the village opposite the church.

POINTS OF INTEREST:

The Church of St Mary the Virgin, Great Eversden – Built in 1466 this church is of the Perpendicular style of English Gothic architecture and has a fine spiked tower.
Cobbs Wood Farm – A typical local farm, but particularly interesting for the walker as each field has information on its crop, previous crop, etc.
Wimpole Hall, Old Wimpole – Due to its size and setting, the house (which is about $^1/_2$ mile off route) is arguably the most impressive country mansion in Cambridgeshire. Built in the 17th and 18th centuries of red brick, the house has had many additions and alterations, but is still breathtaking. It is open to the public from April to October.
St Andrew's Church, Orwell – The church is built from pebble and clunch rubble, the clunch having been quarried in the village. Building having taken place in the 12th, 13th and 14th centuries, the church is an interesting mixture of architectural styles.
St Helen's Church, Little Eversden – Built mostly in the 1400s, this small church is in the Decorated English Gothic style, and has an interesting interior including Victorian Chancel Stalls of the same design and style as those in the Chapel of Queen's College, Cambridge.

REFRESHMENTS:
The Chequers Inn, Orwell.
The Hoops Inn, Great Eversden.

Walk 19   ST NEOTS   6m (10km)

Maps: OS Sheets Landranger 153; Pathfinder 980 and 981.
Linking the Great Ouse River and Paxton Pits.
Start: At 179601, the Great River Ouse car park, St Neots.

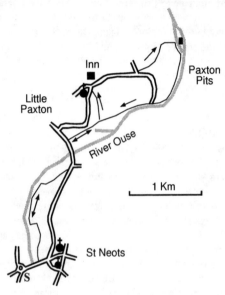

From the car park, near the centre of St Neots, beside the **Great River Ouse** walk to the river then under the road bridge to the left, and up on to the road. Cross the river towards St Neots, then turn first left (signed for the library) and follow the right-hand fork towards Waitrose. Take the footpath on the left after the first, smaller, car park, but before the larger one, and, at its end, continue down an alley. At the end of the alley, go ahead, along Priory Road. At the corner, cross the stile ahead and go diagonally left across a field to a gate. Walk along the left-hand edge of the field beyond to reach the river. Turn right to walk beside the river. On reaching a small wood, turn right along its outside edge, and then, at the gate in the corner, turn left along a fence to a road. Cross, with care, and turn left. Cross the footpath bridge over the river – the two arms of the river are separated by a mill and meadow – to Little Paxton. Turn right along the riverside path, following it behind the gardens to reach **Paxton Pits Nature Reserve**. Take the path on the left along the outside of the Reserve to reach a road in the village. Turn right to a three-way road junction. Turn left to visit **St James' Church**, and right to continue the walk. Go along the road until it ends in a Reserve car park. Continue ahead, then take the left-hand fork into the Reserve. (The right-hand fork can be taken for a slightly shorter walk through the Reserve.) Follow the path for about $\frac{1}{2}$ mile to reach a path junction. Take the path to the right, signed for the Great Ouse Way to Little Paxton and St Neots, following it to the river. Go around to the right, then follow the path for about 2 miles now, re-entering the Reserve and exiting it where you first reached it on the outward route. Now retrace your outward route back to **St Neots**.

POINTS OF INTEREST:
Great Ouse River – The Great Ouse River Valley provides some of the most interesting and attractive countryside in the county. In the county's expanse of dry arable land, the river and the nearby water-filled gravel pits provide a rare and valuable habitat for water species – reeds, rushes and marshplants; dragonflies and butterflies; coots, moorhens, swans, etc. In addition, the river flood meadows provide a permanent grassland habitat rich in mature trees and wild flower species such as cowslip, crosswort and salad burnet.
Paxton Pits Nature Reserve – Created by the filling of disused gravel pits, Paxton Pits provides a very valuable habitat for wetland species. It is particularly important for its wildfowl, and is home to one of the largest inland cormorant colonies in Britain. The Reserve is a Site of Special Scientific Interest, but is still very accessible, and includes a visitor centre, nature trails and various bird hides.
St James' Church, Little Paxton – This church is a mix of the Norman and Perpendicular styles of architecture – the nave and chancel are definitely Norman and the tower is definitely Perpendicular.
St Neots – Initially the site of a Benedictine Priory dating from the 900s, St Neots is an ancient town with many points of historical interest: St Mary's Church is one of the biggest and most representative of late medieval churches in the county; the Market Place, with its central 19th-century pillar and surrounding, fine 17th- and 18th-century houses; and the Victorian Congregational Church on the High Street.

REFRESHMENTS:
The Anchor, Little Paxton.
St Neots has numerous possibilities.

41

Walk 20   **ELY**   6m (10km)

Maps: OS Sheets Landranger 143; Pathfinder 941 and 961.

The countryside around Ely, including some fine views of the Cathedral.

Start: At 540803, Ely Cathedral.

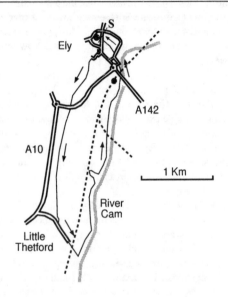

Standing outside the main entrance of **Ely Cathedral**, with your back to it, turn left and walk along the road past Kings School to reach a road junction. Take the diagonal path opposite, following it through Kings School Barlow Farm. Now follow the road right, left and right again, then take the path beside the tennis courts up on to an embankment. Turn left and follow the path along the embankment to a stile. Go over and head straight across the golf course (diagonally, as waymarked). At the far side of the golf course, take the signed path through the hedge to reach the main road (the A142). Cross, with care, and continue straight ahead along a grassy track, initially along the driveway to the business park. Continue ahead along a lovely shaded path, following it beside and across several fields. Continue along the edge of a garden and down a drive to reach a road at Little Thetford.

Turn left and walk through Little Thetford to reach the railway line. Cross, with care, and, at the end of the tarmac lane, go up on to an embankment. Turn left and follow the path on the embankment beside the **River Cam** towards Ely. About half-way to the town you will need to do a slight detour to the left to cross a large irrigation channel joining the river.

On reaching the A142, cross, with care, and turn slightly right to rejoin the riverside path. Follow the path to reach the Old Boathouse Cafe and the Cutters Inn. Walk along the left-hand side of the inn towards the car park, then, maintaining the same general direction, follow the small alley beside the car park. At the end, walk along Jubilee Terrace (passing Hereward Housing) to reach the main road. Turn right and walk to the black signpost on the other side of the street. Now turn left and walk through a park. At the top of the park, walk along the lane to reach the Cathedral. You may either enter the Cathedral here and leave by the main entrance, or walk through the grounds, around to the right, to reach the main entrance. Ahead, across the green, is **Oliver Cromwell's House** and the Tourist Information Office.

POINTS OF INTEREST:

Ely Cathedral – Set on the Isle of Ely, standing far above the rest of the town, the Cathedral was built from 1081-1189 on the site of an ancient monastery. It is a superb example of Romanesque architecture. Take particular note of the beautiful Octagon which replaced the collapsed Norman tower, the 14th-cenrtury Lady Chapel and its carvings, the Prior's Door and the lovely painted ceiling of the Nave.

River Cam – The River Cam, a tributary of the Great Ouse River, is one of the most beautiful and atmospheric rivers in England. Meandering through the dry and flat farmland of the fens, the river provides a striking contrast, both in scenery and in its wildlife, this ranging from reeds to water-lilies, pondskaters to kingfishers. Due to its popularity, the river is also well-endowed with delightful riverside inns and teashops, and a variety of excellent boating opportunities.

Oliver Cromwell's House, Ely – This 17th-century house, once the home of Oliver Cromwell, one of England's most famous and powerful leaders, has recently been extensively restored and gives an excellent insight into life in Cromwell's times.

REFRESHMENTS:

Ely has possibilities to suit all tastes and budgets, but does specialise in tea-rooms.

Walk 21   **HUNTINGDON**   6m (10km)

Maps: OS Sheets Landranger 153; Pathfinder 960 and 981.
A very pretty linear walk along the Great Ouse River.
Start: At 238718, the Market Place, Huntingdon.

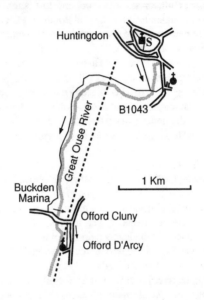

Facing the War Monument, next to **All Saints' Church**, cross the square and turn left
up Market Hill, passing the Tourist Information Office, to reach the ring road. Cross,
with care, and follow Mill Common under the road bridge to its end. Cross **Portholme
Meadow** along the path ahead, for Godmanchester, to reach a riverside path. Turn
left and cross the bridge into Godmanchester. To visit the **Church of St Mary** cross
the main road (the B1043), turn right and take the next road on the left.

     To continue the walk retrace your steps to the Great Ouse River and Portholme
Meadow. Cross the meadow along the Ouse Valley Way, the path on your left (not
back to the town) to reach a railway bridge. Follow the track under the railway,
continuing along it for about ¹/₂ mile to reach another track. Turn left and, at the end
of the track, continue ahead along the footpath, following it beside the river for almost
3 miles, crossing a brook about mid-way, to reach Buckden Marina. Continue along

the Ouse Valley Way, going through the holiday cottages and down the drive to a road. Turn left and walk along the road, crossing the railway with care, to reach **All Saints' Church, Offord Cluny**. Retrace your steps a little and take the path on the left immediately before the railway crossing, following it to the small green in Offord D'Arcy. From the green, maintain direction along the road and take the next road on the right to **St Peter's Church**.

To return to Huntingdon take the bus which runs every two hours on weekdays and four hours on Saturdays from the small green in Offord D'Arcy.

POINTS OF INTEREST:

All Saints' Church, Huntingdon – A large, essentially Perpendicular church, with some Norman and Early English aspects. The tower was rebuilt after the Civil War and the very top of it is Victorian. The church has some excellent stained glass windows.
Portholme Meadow – This is one of the largest meadows in England. Roman remains have been found here. The meadow was a racecourse in the time of Cromwell and an airfield in the early days of aviation. It now provides a habitat to many meadowland species. In winter it frequently floods and is visited by migratory birds, including Bewick swans, grey-lag geese and golden plover. The meadow is a registered Site of Special Scientific Interest.
St Mary's Church, Godmanchester – Predominantly Perpendicular, though the chancel is Early English and the west tower, though Perpendicular in appearance, was actually built in 1623, replacing a 13th-century tower. Godmanchester was a Roman settlement and an important medieval centre, and has a number of other fine buildings.
All Saints' Church, Offord Cluny – Built of cobbles, this is a mainly Perpendicular style church, though parts date from the 13th century. Look out for the carved figures in the nave.
St Peter's Church, Offord D'Arcy – A mixture of Norman, 13th-century and English Gothic styles of architecture, the church is very attractive in appearance and houses a lot of interesting monuments.

REFRESHMENTS:
The Black Bull, Godmanchester.
The White Hart Inn, Godmanchester.
The Royal Oak, Godmanchester.
The Swan Inn, Offord Cluny.
The Horseshoe Inn, Offord D'Arcy.

Walk 22   CAMBRIDGE AND WATERBEACH   6¹/₂m (10¹/₂km)

Maps: OS Sheets Landranger 154; Pathfinder 1004 and 982.

A picturesque linear walk along the famous Cambridge to Ely path.

Start: At 445591, Cambridge Castle, Cambridge.

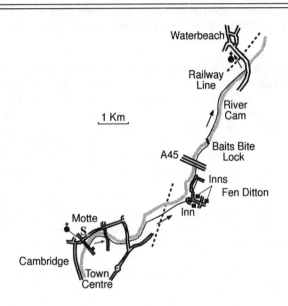

From **Cambridge Castle**, join the main road and walk downhill into the town. Maintain direction to reach the **River Cam**. Cross the river and immediately turn left. Now follow the riverbank for about 1 mile, passing shops, Jesus Green, Midsummer Common, and then passing under a road bridge to reach the corner of Abbey Road. Walk ahead, along the road (following the cycle signs to Barnwell Road), then, at the end, follow the signed Fen Rivers Way towards Fen Ditton and Ely, crossing the railway on the way.

On reaching a lane end, turn right and walk to **St Mary's Church, Fen Ditton**. Now take the road on the left, passing the **Almshouses**, on your right, and walk to the corner. Here, take the signed footpath ahead, rejoining the Fen Rivers Way. Follow the Way across a playing field then along the edge of a field to reach a lane. Turn left to reach a road. Turn right and walk to the end of the road. Now go ahead along a footpath, following it across a field to reach a house, then going diagonally across the next field to return to the river. Now follow the path beside the river towards Baits Bite Lock, going around a large building and veering right, off Fen Rivers Way, to reach the lock.

At the lock, cross the river and continue beside the river, heading in the same direction as before, for almost 2 miles to reach a road and the Riverside Inn. Turn left and walk along the road for about a mile to reach the village green at the centre of Waterbeach, passing St John's Church and the Baptist Church on your left.

From the village green, buses return to Cambridge approximately every 30 minutes on weekdays, every hour on Saturdays and every four hours on Sundays.

POINTS OF INTEREST:

Cambridge Castle – The Castle was built in 1068 by William the Conqueror and then expanded considerably around 1300 by Edward I, who added a gatehouse, towers, a great hall and a chapel. This was the peak of the castle's life: by 1606 most of the stone had been taken for college buildings and only the gatehouse remained. Now the castle consists solely of the original motte (about 200ft in diameter), but the site still commands an excellent view of the city.

River Cam – The Cam, a tributary of the Great Ouse River, is one of the most beautiful and atmospheric of rivers in England. Meandering through the dry, flat farmland of the fens, the river provides a striking contrast both in scenery and in its wildlife, this ranging from reeds to water-lilies, pondskaters to kingfishers. Due to its popularity, the river also has many delightful riverside inns and teashops, and a number of excellent boating opportunities.

St Mary's Church, Fen Ditton – The church is mainly 14th-century, though the very impressive tower is not of this time.

Almshouses, Fen Ditton – This small row of houses were originally built in 1665 by the Willys Family as six almshouses. They were rebuilt in 1877 by Thomas Bailey and used as an infirmary.

REFRESHMENTS:

The Riverside Inn, Clayhithe.

The Sun Inn, Waterbeach.

The White Horse, Waterbeach.

There is also a huge range of possibilities in Cambridge.

Walk 23   EARITH   7m (11km)

Maps: OS Sheets Landranger 142; Pathfinder 960.

The merging of the town and the countryside. Best on a Sunday.

Start: At 386748, in High Street, Earith.

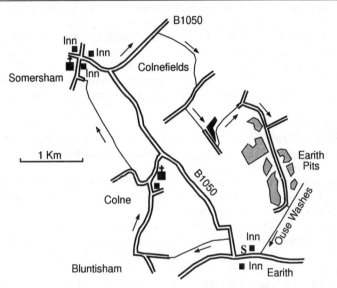

Walk west along the High Street (the A1123), then take the road for Somersham (the B1050). After about 200 yards, just before the last building on the left, turn left along the footpath for Bluntisham, going through orchards, grazing land and several fields to reach a lane. Continue along the lane to reach a road. Bluntisham is about ¹/₂ mile to the left, but the walk turns right, then right again at the next road junction. Follow the pavement into Colne, arriving at the village green and **St Helen's Church**. Cross the green opposite the church and go along Old Church Road, following it around a sharp right corner and continuing to the farm ahead. There, take the signed footpath across and around fields into Somersham. On reaching a raised track, go straight over and continue along the path to reach a lane. Turn left, and, at the end, turn right, passing **St John's Church** to reach the main road at the centre of Somersham.

Turn right and follow the Chatteris road to reach a junction. Continue along the road towards Chatteris (the B1050), going straight on, with great care (or following the smaller road over the top while the main road has no verges or pavement). Continue towards Chatteris until the road bends to the left. Here there are a footpath and a bridge to your right: follow the path along the edges of several fields and then through a shaded area. When the shaded path finishes, take the grassy track to the right, following it around to the left, then to the right to join a gravelled track. Follow this track for about $^1/_2$ mile then turn left along a footpath. Follow the path along the edges of several fields to reach **Earith Pits** and a track. Maintain direction (do not turn right), following the track through the pit ponds, and continuing along it as it turns gradually to the right. Beyond the ponds, walk past several large warehouses, then, when the track makes a definite right turn, turn left to the **Ouse Washes**, joining the Ouse Washes Bridleway. On the top of the embankment, turn right and walk beside the washes to reach Earith Bridge. Turn right and return to Earith along the High Street.

POINTS OF INTEREST:

St Helen's Church, Colne – The church was built at the end of the 19th century using the stone of its predecessor. The church has a tower and a lead spike, and houses a very pretty organ and organ case.

St John's Church, Somersham – The church is built almost completely in the Early English style, possibly due to the ease of funds and a need for perfection as Somersham was once a palace town for the Bishops of Ely.

Earith Pits – Created as a side effect of local industry, these are a series of disused gravel pits that have since filled with water and now provide a valuable wetland habitat for numerous insects and birds. Some of the pits are also used for fishing and are private or club-owned.

Ouse Washes – The Ouse Washes, registered as a 'Special Protection Area' were created by the draining of the Fens and the forming of the Old and New Bedford Rivers. Managed as agricultural washland that seasonally floods the area has a huge diversity of natural species, some of which are quite rare. The area is particularly valuable to waterfowl, providing sanctuary for over 20,000 birds, including breeding populations of Ruff, Bewick Swan, Whooper Swan and Hen Harrier as well as many migratory waders.

REFRESHMENTS:

The Riverview Inn, Earith.
The Crown Inn, Earith.
The Green Man, Colne.
Rose and Crown, Somersham.
The George, Somersham.

Walk 24   **BENSONS FEN**   7m (11km)

Maps: OS Sheets Landranger 142; Pathfinder 919, 940, 941 and 920.

Pleasant fenland country, and some waterlife.

Start: At 400905, St Mary's Church, Doddington.

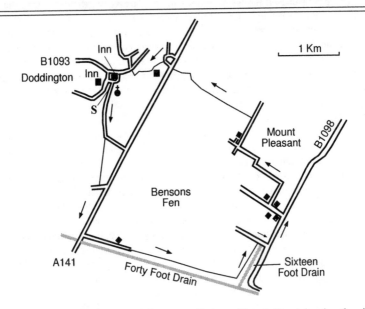

From **St Mary's Church**, Doddington, walk down Church Street, leaving the village and taking the right-hand fork at the end to continue down a farm track. At the farm, walk along the right-hand side of the farm buildings, then maintain direction between a drain and a fence, going along the edge of the field. Go straight across the next two fields to reach a track. Turn left to reach the main road (the A141). Turn right, with care, and follow the path beside the road to reach a bridge over the **Forty Foot Drain**. Cross the road, with care, and, immediately before crossing the bridge, drop down the embankment to reach a small lane running underneath the bridge. Turn left and walk along this lane by the side of the drain for about $^1/_2$ mile to reach the end of the track. Maintain direction along a path, but walking now on top of the drain's embankment. Follow the path to the Sixteen Foot Drain, on the left. Follow the path around to the left and follow the new drain to reach a tarmac lane and a bridge. Cross the bridge to the B1098 and turn left, with care, maintaining direction to reach the next bridge. Here, cross back over Sixteen Foot Drain then follow the right-hand track ahead, going around in front of a house, then around a series of left and right bends to reach another house. Now go along the track to the right, following it until it makes a slight left-hand wiggle. Here, on the left of the second ditch, take the footpath along the edges of two fields. Go straight across the next field and then along the edges of two more to reach a road (the A141). Cross, with care, and turn right along the road to reach a lane on the left. Go down the lane to a corner and cross a bridge into the field on your left, walk along its right-hand edge. Cross the bridge at the end, go through an orchard and around the edge of the field at the end (this section is slightly overgrown) to reach a driveway. Turn right, then right again down a road to reach the main road (the B1093). Turn left, with care, to return to Doddington: the church is reached by taking the first turn left, then going left again.

POINTS OF INTEREST:

St Mary's Church, Doddington – The church is mainly 14th-century, although it seems to have been started earlier and some parts were not completed until the early 15th century. The most notable features are the excellent 15th-century windows in the chancel, though there is much inside the church that is very interesting.

Forty Foot Drain – Although a man-made feature, this wide channel of water in an otherwise rather dry landscape has become a natural habitat for a wide variety of water species including many reeds, rushes and marsh plants, a number a species of insect, most notably dragonflies and butterflies, and a variety of birds including coots, moorhens and swans. The embankments are also home to a great variety and abundance of wild flowers.

REFRESHMENTS:
The George Inn, Doddington.
The Three Tuns Inn, Doddington.

Walk 25   BURWELL   7m (11km)

Maps: OS Sheets Landranger 154; Pathfinder 982.

An interesting walk with a prehistoric feel.

Start: At 589661, St Mary the Virgin's Church, Burwell.

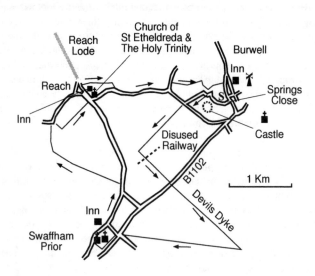

From the front entrance of the **Church of St Mary the Virgin**, walk down Springs Close, turning left to reach **Burwell Castle**. Walk through the site, keeping to the right to rejoin Springs Close. Turn left almost immediately to follow a path across fields to reach a road. Cross and follow the public byway ahead for $\frac{1}{2}$ mile to reach **Devil's Dyke**. Turn left along the dyke, following the embankment path (leaving it twice: once to cross an old railway line and once to cross a road – the B1102, please cross with care). Go past a path to the left, then cross a stile to reach a small path to the right. Take this, following it diagonally across fields to reach the main road (the B1102) at a junction. Walk down Clay Hill opposite Swaffham Prior, and turn first left to reach the **Church of St Cyriac and St Julitta** and the **Church of St Mary.**

Walk through the churchyard to reach the main road in Swaffham Prior. Turn right and follow the road for almost a mile, right out of town, to reach a signed public byway to the left. Follow this for just over a mile, bearing to the right towards the end.

At the end, walk down the track ahead and then take the public byway on your right up a slight hill. Having passed two fields, take the well-trodden path to your left, following it to a track and continuing into the village of Reach, arriving opposite the **Church of St Etheldreda and the Holy Trinity.** Cross the green to the farther road and walk to the left. At the end of the road, go over the stile to **Reach Lode**, walking beside a fir-tree fence and along a very broad public byway. Follow the byway to a road. Turn left along the road for about $^1/_2$ mile to reach a junction. Now follow the public footpath into Burwell. (If waters are high it would be advisable to walk along the road to the left a little, taking the next signed path.) On arriving at the recreation ground/green, walk down the road, beside it to the right and into the village. To reach the **Stevens Mill and Burwell Museum**, turn left, then take the first turning right.

POINTS OF INTEREST:

Church of St Mary the Virgin, Burwell – The church is regarded as the best example of the Perpendicular style in the county.

Burwell Castle, Burwell – Work on the castle began in 1144 but was never completed, though the remains of a stone keep, curtain walls and a wide, wet moat are visible.

Devil's Dyke – The Dyke is often considered the most impressive archaeological monument in Cambridgeshire. At 30 yards wide, and 5 yards deep it is the largest such structure in Britain, though not the longest. It is 16km long, running from Reach to Woodditton, cutting the Icknield Way – the chalkland thoroughfare through the waterlogged fens in prehistoric times. It was built to halt the progress of the Danes.

St Cyriac's and St Julitta's Church, Swaffham Prior – Now redundant and unfortunately decaying. However, the medieval tower is still very pretty.

St Mary's Church, Swaffham Prior – The church has an unusual second stage to the tower, being octagonal. It also has some good brasses and stained-glass windows.

Church of St Etheldreda and the Holy Trinity, Reach – Built in 1860 this squat church is considered by some to be one of the most ugly of all Victorian churches.

Reach Lode – The Lode was a Roman irrigation channel running for just under 3 miles from the end of the Devil's Dyke at Reach to the River Cam at Upware.

Stevens Mill and Burwell Museum – Just behind the main street of Burwell, Stevens Mill was still working until relatively recently. It is still intact and is now a museum.

REFRESHMENTS:
The Crown, Burwell.
The Five Bells, Burwell.
The Red Lion, Swaffham Prior.
The King Inn, Reach.

Walk 26   **WICKEN**   7m (11km)

Maps: OS Sheets Landranger 154; Pathfinder 961 and 982.

A wetland habitats walk, with marsh, river and manmade drain.

Start: At 571707, the Maids Head Inn, Wicken.

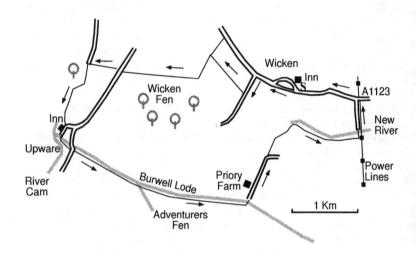

From the inn, on the Village Green, at the centre of Wicken, walk westwards along the main road (the A1123) to reach a road signed for **Wicken Fen** on the left. Go along this road for about 500 yards to reach a public byway, on the right just after the National Trust car park. Follow the byway for $^1/_2$ mile to reach a path at a T-junction. Turn left, following the path beside Wicken Fen to reach a road. Cross and follow the track/wide footpath opposite through a field to reach a grassy, tree-lined track. Turn left and walk beside woodland. At the far corner of the wood, follow the path around to the right and, at the edge of the field, turn left to follow the field edge around to a stile. Cross and keep to the right-hand edge of a horse field to reach a road in Upware.

Turn right and follow the road past the inn to reach a path beside the **River Cam**. Follow this path to a road, crossing straight over to follow a path beside **Burwell**

Lode. Follow the path for about 2 miles to reach a bridge and a lifting bridge. Turn left at the bridge and walk down the lane past Priory Farm. When the lane ends, maintain direction along the footpath, eventually to New River and a small bridge. Turn right either before or after crossing the bridge as there are paths on both banks of the river. Follow the path to reach a small bridge directly under the electricity lines. Turn left (crossing the bridge if you did not cross earlier) and follow a track up to the main road (the A1123). Turn left, with care, to reach **St Lawrence's Church**, continuing along the road to return to Wicken and the start.

POINTS OF INTEREST:

Wicken Fen – The Fen is a National Nature Reserve owned by the National Trust and is one of the most important wetland habitats in Britain. Surrounded by such a dry and intensely farmed land, the 600 acre wetland (originally part of the Great Fen Levels) provides a vital habitat for numerous plant, insect and mammal species. Marked walks, hides and watchtowers are provided, as is detailed information on the site and its wildlife, with further information and displays on the history of the area. There is an entry fee for the Reserve. Note that the Reserve has only one entrance/exit i.e. you can not walk through it.

River Cam – The Cam, a tributary of the Great Ouse River, is one of the most beautiful and atmospheric of rivers in England. Meandering through the dry, flat farmland of the fens, the river provides a striking contrast both in scenery and in its wildlife, this ranging from reeds to water-lilies, pondskaters to kingfishers. Due to its popularity, the river also has many delightful riverside inns and teashops, and a number of excellent boating opportunities.

Burwell Lode – Although a manmade feature, this channel of water in an otherwise rather dry landscape has become a natural habitat for a wide diversity of water species including many reeds, rushes and marsh plants, dragonflies and butterflies, and coots, moorhens and swans. The embankments are also home to a great variety and abundance of wild flowers.

St Lawrence's Church, Wicken – A small, secluded church almost hidden by trees. It dates from the 14th century and has a more impressive interior than would be expected.

REFRESHMENTS:
The Maids Head, Wicken.
The Five Miles From Anywhere, No Hurry Inn, Upware.

Walk 27   **LINTON**   7m (11km)

Maps: OS Sheets Landranger 154; Pathfinder 1027.

A very pleasant walk visiting some pretty villages and interesting churches.

Start: At 559467, in High Street, Linton.

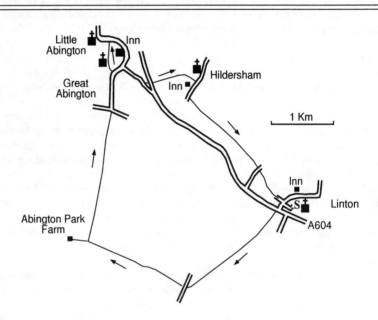

Walk southwards along the High Street in Linton: **St Mary the Virgin's Church** is about 200 yards down the small side street on your right, in a very picturesque setting near the river and ford. Continue along the High Street to reach the A604. Turn right, and, after about 200 yards, cross, with care, and take the footpath, on the left, signed for Chesterton. Follow the path across fields for just over a mile to reach a track. Go straight across, then take the path in the further field, following it (as indicated) for just over a mile to reach a concrete road. Turn right and follow this road/track to reach a road in Great Abington. Maintain direction up the High Street and, after about 500 yards, take the signed path on the left to **St Mary's Church, Great Abington**.

At the church, take the path beside the churchyard, following it to reach a ro⸀⸀ ⸀⸀ Little Abington. Turn left to visit **St Mary's Church, Little Abington**. The walk turns right. Follow the road around to the right to reach the road for Linton and Hildersham, on the left, just beyond the inn. Follow this road for about 500 yards, then take the footpath, on the left, beside the house, for Hildersham. Follow this well-trodden path to the A604. Cross, with care, and continue along the path, crossing fields and paddocks to reach a road in Hildersham. Turn left for about 200 yards to visit **Holy Trinity Church**, or turn right to continue the walk. After 200 yards, turn left along a signed path opposite the inn, following it towards Linton. Go straight across a lane going to your right and straight across a tarmac path. Then, where the path becomes tarmaced and forks, take the right-hand branch. Go across a small road, then pass Shepherd's Hall to reach the High Street in Linton and the end of the walk.

POINTS OF INTEREST:

St Mary the Virgin's Church, Linton – Dating from the late 13th and 14th centuries, this large church is mainly in the Early English architectural style, though the later parts are Decorated English Gothic and there are also some Perpendicular additions.
St Mary's Church, Great Abington – Mostly of Early English style architecture, this church was built mainly in the 13th century but does have some 14th-century features – the four-bay arcade separating the nave and the south aisle, and a tower arch.
St Mary's Church, Little Abington – Built of flint and rubble, this church in English Gothic style dates mainly from the early 14th century, though it was partially restored in the 19th century.
Holy Trinity Church, Hildersham – The church has a fine (though perhaps rather gloomy) interior and houses several unusual monuments, and a 13th-century oak ladder which runs up the inside of the tower.
Linton – The village has a number of fine buildings including Chandlers and the Bell Inn, both on the High Street, which are pre-reformation, and Linton House, dated 1710, in Town Lane.

REFRESHMENTS:
The Dog and Duck, Linton.
The Crown Inn, Linton.
The Green Hill, Linton.
The Three Tuns, Great Abington.
The Peartree, Hildersham.

Maps: OS Sheets Landranger 153; Pathfinder 1026.

Typical Cambridgeshire countryside and villages.

Start: At 310428, St Catherine's Church, Litlington.

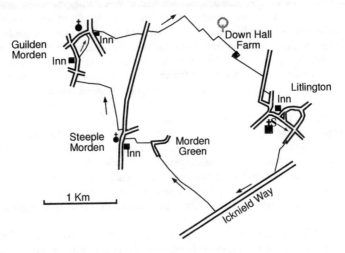

From **St Catherine's Church** walk down the road into Litlington and take the second road on the right signed as a footpath to Steeple Morden. Walk past the houses and continue along a track, following it around to the left to reach a line of trees and a track (Icknield Way). Turn right along the Icknield Way for almost a mile, passing **Whitethorn Wood**. Just over the brow of the (very small) hill turn right along a footpath, crossing two fields, then going around the edge of a garden to the house. On the other side of the house, cross the signed stile to the left and follow a path through the garden. Turn right along the edge of the garden to reach a field. Turn right, but, soon, left to reach a grassy track. Turn right and follow the track to reach a road in Morden Green. Go ahead to the corner, then take the footpath on the left – diverted from in front of the house to around the garage, then across the garden to a stile. Cross and follow the well-trodden path beside a clump of trees, then diagonally across a field (via the small clump of undergrowth in the middle) to reach a stile in the fence, by the farm. Cross and follow the farm drive to a lane. Turn left to reach the main road in Steeple Morden. Turn right, then take the footpath on the other side of **St Peter**

and St Paul's Church, following it beside some gardens. Turn right along the backs of the houses to reach a track. Turn right slightly, then continue as before between the houses and a bowling green to reach a road. Go through the car park to a gate and follow the well-trodden path beyond diagonally across a field. Turn right at the bottom to walk beside a brook. At the end of the path, turn left along an obvious path across a field. At the top of the field, take the small alley ahead, between the gardens, to reach a road. Turn right into Guilden Morden (winner of the 'Best Kept Village in Cambridgeshire' Award in 1995). At the Three Tuns Inn, turn right along a byway and then a road to reach the **church**. Turn right to a road junction. Take the footpath along the left side of the Edward VII Inn, then go diagonally across two playing fields to the corner just beyond the children's play area. Cross a stile, turn right and follow the field edge to the corner. Turn left along the field edge to a road. Cross, bearing left slightly to take the path ahead, following it across a field to a bridge. Cross and follow the field edge to the hedge, go along a track for 20 yards, then turn right. Now follow the track ahead for about $^1/_2$ mile (with a slight kink to the left in the middle) to reach the end of a wood and a track. Turn left, then take the path on the right to Down Hall Farm. At the farm, follow the roadway around the corner to the right, then take the path along the nearside of the far building (a watermill) on the left. Follow the path through the garden then across a field to a road. Turn right to reach a footpath on the left, following it across a field to a track. Turn right to return to the church.

POINTS OF INTEREST:

St Catherine's Church, Litlington – An elegant church in Decorated style, but with several Perpendicular style windows. Look out for the blue stained-glass window donated to the church in remembrance of the Second World War.

Whitethorn Wood – Planted in 1994 by the Woodland Trust, this small wood contains a host of tree species natural to the area. The name derives from a legend that Robin Hood once shot an arrow of whitethorn here which subsequently sprouted into a tree.

St Peter and St Paul's Church, Steeple Morden – Originally with a steeple after which the village was named, lost during (unfortunate) rebuilding around 1800.

St Mary's Church, Guilden Morden – A large church with a broad square tower and lead spire. Its date of construction is difficult to assess with certainty.

REFRESHMENTS:

The Crown, Litlington.
Waggon and Horses, Steeple Morden.
The Three Tuns, Guilden Morden.
Edward VII, Guilden Morden.

Maps: OS Sheets Landranger 142; Pathfinder 897.
A very pleasant walk through the Cambridgeshire countryside.
Start: At 122055, St Botolph's Church, Helpston.

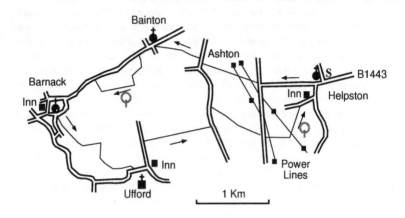

From **St Botolph's Church, Helpston** walk westwards along the main road (the B1443) for about $^1/_2$ mile to reach a sharp right-hand corner. Here, take the signed path straight ahead, following it diagonally across two fields to reach a stile in the corner of the second. Cross and follow the obvious, and wide, Torpel Way to reach a road in Ashton. Turn right (leaving the Torpel Way), then take the footpath on the left, following it diagonally across a field, and then around several small fields linked by stiles. Go around the edge of a larger field, cross the stile on your left mid-way along the fence. Follow the well-trodden path beyond through the undergrowth to reach a stile ahead/slightly right. Follow the signed path beyond along the right-hand edge of a field to reach a footbridge. Cross and turn left along the edge of a field to reach a chicken farm. Turn right immediately before the buildings and walk to a road. Turn left into **Bainton**, passing Blue Boar House, St Mary's Church and the village cross. Continue past the telephone box and take the next path on the left. Follow this signed path between the houses, then turn right beside a dyke and walk to the end of the wide, grassy track. Turn left along a field edge then, on the far side of the field, turn right along the Torpel Way, following it along the field edge and through woodland. At the end of the woods, turn right following the Torpel Way to a road. Turn left into Barnack. After almost 500 yards take the road on the left, passing the **Methodist Church** on your right and continuing to the **Church of St John the Baptist**. The inn is a further 100 yards along the road. Take the path opposite the church, beside the Post Office, following it around the back of the gardens and along several field edges to reach a track. Turn right, following the track to the far side of a clump of trees. Now take the signed path on the left along the edge of the field. Go around the field edge (at points seemingly going back on yourself) to reach a road. Turn left into Ufford. **St Andrew's Church** is on the right as you reach the centre of the village. At the road junction in front of the inn, turn left. Follow the road for about 500 yards to reach a lane on the right, just after Honeysuckle Cottage. Take this, following the path at its end straight ahead for almost a mile to reach a road. Turn left for almost 200 yards, then take the signed track on the right, following it for just under a mile to reach a road. Cross and take the bridleway opposite, following it to the edge of a wood. Here, turn left along a path, following it to a road. Turn right to a junction, then turn left, passing **John Clare's Cottage**, to return to the start.

POINTS OF INTEREST:

St Botolph's Church, Helpston – Mainly Saxon and Norman in style, the church was probably built in the 12th century, though the tower was rebuilt in 1865.

Bainton – The lovely Blue Boar Cottage was built in 1803. St Mary's Church, a tall church with a spire and a bellflower frieze, dates from the 13th century, and is mainly in the Decorated style. The Village Cross, in the centre of the village, next to the church is a pyramid of four large stone steps.

Methodist Church, Barnack – An old Wesleyan Church dating from 1898.

Church of St John the Baptist, Barnack – Having been built through numerous eras and in several styles this is a very interesting church. Some even consider it to be one of the most pleasing churches in the county. The earliest work is Saxon.

St Andrew's Church, Ufford – In the Decorated and Perpendicular styles, and containing an interesting range of artefacts, including two medieval bells.

John Clare's Cottage, Helpston – This is the cottage in which John Clare, the famous poet, was born in 1793.

REFRESHMENTS:

The Exeter Arms, Helpston.
The Blue Bell Inn, Helpston.
The Fox Inn, Barnack.
Ye Olde White Hart, Ufford.

Walk 30   WOODWALTON AND UPWOOD   7¹/₂m (12km)

Maps: OS Sheets Landranger 142; Pathfinder 940.

A fine walk through three fenland villages.

Start: At 214808, on the Village Green, opposite the Elephant and Castle Inn, Woodwalton.

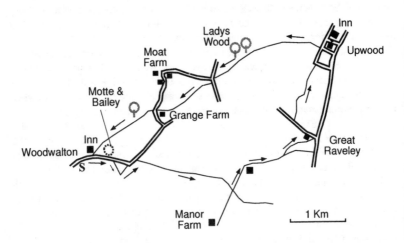

From Woodwalton Green, walk down the main road towards Great Raveley for about 500 yards, and, a little after the slight corner, take the signed footpath to your right. Walk uphill beside the field edge, then maintain direction across the next field to reach a track at the top of the ridge. Turn left and follow the track to a road. Continue ahead along the road to reach a bridleway on the right. Follow the bridleway beside fields for about 1¹/₄ miles to reach the junction of four hedges, and a narrow footpath on the right, coming from Manor Farm. Turn left and follow the footpath away from Manor Farm, crossing a field towards the left-hand side of a barn. At the barn, turn right (eastwards) along a track, following it to the lowest point of the local area, where two hedges cross. Here, turn left, off the track, and follow a field edge, keeping a hedge on your right, to the end of the field. Turn right and follow a drain along the top of the field for about 75 yards, then turn left over a bridge. Take the obvious path ahead across the field, and turn right along a track, following it to the road in Great Raveley.

Turn left along the road, then take the signed public footpath on the right, passing houses and gardens and then going through fields and over stiles to reach Upwood village. Take care in the third field where the path veers around the top of the field to reach a bridge and stile midway along the top hedge. In Upwood, walk ahead, along the main road (High Street) for about 800 yards to reach the church and the inn on the right.

Reverse your route along the road to reach a signed footpath on the right, following it through a housing estate to reach the edge of the village. Follow the signed path across fields and stiles, and then beside Lady's Wood. At the end of the wood, go diagonally across a field to reach a track. Continue along the track to meet another track and turn left to follow this track, passing a track and a public footpath sign, on the right, to reach a gas hydrant and a hole in the fence on the right, indicated as a path by a white paint mark. Follow this path across a field, going around the edges of the next three fields, crossing the bridges between them, to reach another bridge. Cross and follow the obvious path to Grange Farm. At the farm, follow the obvious path, heading south-westwards, uphill, across a field. At the top of the field, drop down into Woodwalton, heading to the right of the trees and to the left of the generator, and passing an **old castle** site to the right.

POINTS OF INTEREST:

St Peter's Church, Upwood – The church has parts dating from the Norman period, most notably the nave and the two windows above it. Most other parts of the church date from the late 12th century, with the exception of the tower which is late 13th-century. The church also has some unusual and interesting monuments, both inside and in the graveyard.

Old Castle, Woodwalton – This was an early Norman motte and bailey castle, the motte being approximately 40 yards in diameter.

REFRESHMENTS:

The Elephant and Castle, Woodwalton.
The Cross Keys, Upwood.

Walk 31   **WARBOYS**   7$^{1}/_{2}$m (12km)

Maps: OS Sheets Landranger 142; Pathfinder 960 and 940.
A linear walk including pretty villages and historic towns.
Start: At 303801, the Clocktower/Market Place, Warboys.

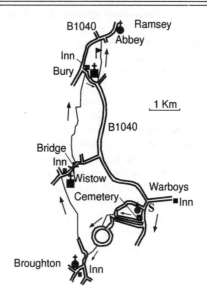

From the Clocktower/Market Place (erected in 1887), walk down the main road towards Huntingdon, passing **St Mary Magdalene's Church**. Immediately after the cemetery, turn right down the signed track, following it to its end. Turn left across a field to join another track and, at the buildings, turn right and follow the track to reach a footpath, on the right, going straight across a field. Take this path across several fields to reach a stile on to a lane. Maintaining direction, walk down the lane into Broughton. At the cross-roads, the church and inn are straight ahead, but the walk turns right along a lane. At its end, cross a stile on the right and cross a field to another stile. Cross and maintain direction to reach a sandy lane. Turn left along the lane and, at its end, follow the shaded path ahead, then follow the waymarkers along field edges to reach a dyke. Bear left and, after one field, cross a field heading to the right of a tall tree. Follow this path to reach a road in Wistow. Turn right and follow the road (towards

Warboys) through the town, passing **St John the Baptist's Church**. Just after the bridge, take the footpath on the left and follow it to the edge of Bury, taking care just after a bridge where the path is not obvious: you need to turn right and follow the field edge. On reaching a sandy, house-lined track, follow it (it becomes tarmac) to reach the main road (the B1040). Turn right, with care, to reach the **Church of the Holy Cross**. Take the signed path through the churchyard, following it beside a golf course to reach the eastern end of the High Street in Ramsey. Turn right for **Ramsey Abbey** and **St Mary's Church**, or turn left for the Market Place and the centre of the town. The return bus to Warboys goes from the Market Place. Buses are every two hours during the week, and every four hours at weekends.

POINTS OF INTEREST:

St Mary Magdalene's Church, Warboys – This is a very grand looking church with a high and impressive tower. Note the interesting door-knocker to the chancel consisting of a lion's head and two fighting dragons.

St John the Baptist's Church, Wistow – The church has been built in such a variety and combination of styles that its actual date remains open. In spite of this mixture, the church is quite pretty and has some marvellous stained-glass windows.

Church of the Holy Cross, Bury – This large, well-kept church is thought to have been built around the 13th century, although precise dates for certain parts have proved rather puzzling.

Ramsey Abbey – The Abbey was founded by Benedictine monks in 969AD and was one of the most important monastic houses in the county right up to the Dissolution. The abbey was then destroyed, its stones being used to build several of the Cambridge colleges and a number of churches in the area. The original Chapel House remained, however. It has had numerous alterations and additions so is rather a mix of styles. It is currently used as a Grammar School. Also on the site is the Gatehouse, a very fine piece of architecture.

St Mary's Church, Ramsey – This very large church was built in 1858 and has some excellent stained-glass windows.

REFRESHMENTS:
The White Hart, Warboys.
The Crown, Broughton.
The Three Horseshoes, Wistow.
The White Lion, Bury.
In addition, Ramsey has something for all tastes and budgets.

Walk 32   **OUSE WASHES**   7¹/₂m (12km)

Maps: OS Sheets Landranger 142; Pathfinder 960 and 961.

A beautiful wetland habitat, and the ideal walk for those who always get lost!

Start: At 395747, the Earith Hermitage Bridge lay-by/car park.

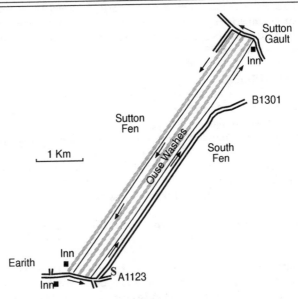

The walk starts from the Hermitage Bridge at Earith (the second bridge reached heading eastwards from Earith along the A1123). Follow the signed public path along the top of the embankment on the right-hand side of the New Bedford River (one of the **Ouse Washes**), heading roughly northwards for just over 3 miles to reach a road and the very picturesque Anchor Inn at Sutton Gault.

At the road, turn left and follow it for about 500 yards to reach the Old Bedford River. Here, turn left along the public footpath running between the river and the drain. Now follow this path for the 3¹/₂ miles or so back to Earith. About half-way along the path a small bridge will give you the option of walking on the other side of the drain (the right-hand bank as opposed to the left).

On meeting the A1123 at the end of the walk, turn left, with care, and follow it for about 500 yards to return to the start. Earith is reached by turning right along the road for about 500 yards.

POINTS OF INTEREST:

Ouse Washes – The Ouse Washes, registered as a 'Special Protection Area' were created by the draining of the Fens and the forming of the Old and New Bedford Rivers. Managed as agricultural washland that seasonally floods the area has a huge diversity of natural species, some of which are quite rare. The area is particularly valuable to waterfowl, providing sanctuary for over 20,000 birds, including breeding populations of Ruff, Bewick Swan, Whooper Swan and Hen Harrier as well as many migratory waders.

REFRESHMENTS:

The Anchor Inn, Sutton Gault.
The Riverview Inn, Earith.
The Crown Inn, Earith.

Walk 33   STETCHWORTH $7^1/_2$m (12km)

Maps: OS Sheets Landranger 154; Pathfinder 1005.

Typical Cambridgeshire countryside and the Stud Farms of Newmarket.

Start: At 641584, a road junction in the centre of Stetchworth.

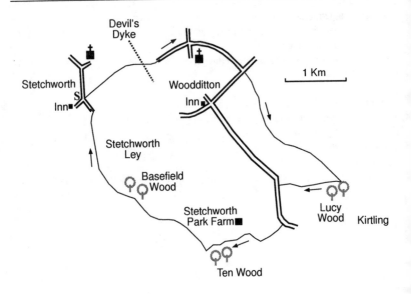

From the central junction of Stetchworth take the footpath signed for Devil's Dyke, going through the houses and continuing beside the line of trees to reach **Devil's Dyke**. Cross the dyke and continue along the path, going diagonally across fields to reach a track. Follow the track straight ahead to reach a road and **St Mary's Church**, Woodditton. Continue along the small road that loops round the back of the church, following it to a T-junction. Go straight across and along the lane opposite. Maintain direction as the lane turns into a track/path, following it to the edge of Lucy Wood. There, turn right and follow the path for about $^1/_2$ mile to reach a road.

Turn left for about 500 yards to reach a footpath on the right. Follow this path straight across several fields, and then along the edge of another field to reach a lane. Turn right towards a farm, and then take the path on the left, walking beside Ten Wood. At the end of the wood, take the path on the right, signed as part of the Stour Valley Way. Follow the path past Basefield Wood. When, at Stetchwood Ley, a small kink in the path occurs just after the wood (a turn to the right, and then to the left), keep heading roughly northwards. When you reach a road, turn left and walk into Stetchworth. **St Peter's Church** is $^1/_2$ mile further along the road.

POINTS OF INTEREST:

St Peter's Church, Stetchworth – Apart from the chancel, which is Early English, the church is almost completely Perpendicular in architectural style, even though it may have been extended in the 19th century.

St Mary's Church, Woodditton – This large church, standing a little way out of the village, is mostly in the Perpendicular style of English Gothic architecture, though there have been additions at later dates.

Devil's Dyke – The Dyke is often considered the most impressive archaeological monument in Cambridgeshire. At 30 yards wide, and 5 yards deep it is the largest such structure in Britain, though not the longest. It is 16km long, running from Reach to Woodditton, cutting the Icknield Way – the chalkland thoroughfare through the waterlogged fens in prehistoric times. It was built to halt the progress of the Danes. The dyke now provides a natural habitat for a variety of plant species including rockrose, milkwort, rest harrow and bellflower. The abundance of butterflies and other insects is also quite amazing at certain times of the year.

REFRESHMENTS:

The Marquis of Granby Inn, Stetchworth.
The Three Blackbirds Inn, Woodditton.

Walk 34   **HARDWICK** $7^1/_2$m (12km)

Maps: OS Sheets Landranger 154; Pathfinder 1003.

Fine countryside, villages and churches, and some equally fine views.

Start: At 374586, St Mary's Church, Hardwick.

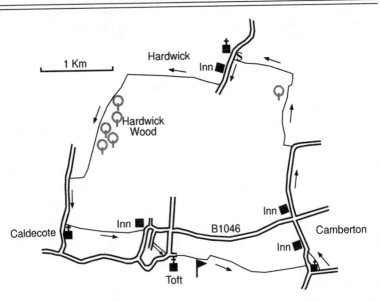

From **St Mary's Church, Hardwick**, walk southwards along the road to reach the end of the buildings. Here, take the bridleway on the right, following it for about a mile. At its end, turn left along the path beside Hardwick Wood. At the end of the path, after just over a mile, follow the bridleway around to the right to reach a road. Turn left to reach the **Church of St Michael and All Angels, Caldecote**.

Take the path through the churchyard, following it through fields, maintaining direction to the last field, where the path goes diagonally left, and then between the houses to reach the main road (the B1046). Turn left, following the road around a right-hand bend. Take the next road on the right, and half-way along it, take the footpath on the left. Follow the path across two fields, heading for the **Church of St Andrew**.

Take the track beside the church, following it across a golf course (beware the golfers and the slight left-hand kink in the path) and then beside several fields to reach a road. Turn right, then take the track beside **St Mary's Church, Comberton** and turn left along the causeway to reach the road again. Bear right along the road into the village centre.

Continue along the road to the B1046. Cross, with care, and take the minor road opposite, following it for just over $^1/_2$ mile. At the sharp right-hand corner, take the path on the left, bearing right with it. Follow this lovely hedged alley, with a fine view of the **Radio Telescopes,** to a small clump of trees. At the trees maintain direction along the track running beside them, then turn left and follow a path across several fields to return to Hardwick.

POINTS OF INTEREST:

St Mary's Church, Hardwick – This church is mostly of the Perpendicular style of English Gothic apart from the tower which seems to date from earlier times, and some of the windows which are decidedly later. Note, also, the particularly fine 15th-century roofs of the nave and chancel.

Church of St Michael and All Angels, Caldecote – This small church is thought to date from the 14th century, but has been much restored, at various times and in various styles.

St Andrew's Church, Toft – Although the original date of this church is uncertain, the tower and north aisle were definitely rebuilt in the 19th century.

St Mary's Church, Comberton – Built in the 14th century, the church is of typical Early English and Perpendicular architectural styles, and has some very pretty decorations and carvings inside.

Radio Telescopes – A technological sculpture erected in 1964, the University's Mullard Radio Telescope exists as three connected, movable receptor dishes.

REFRESHMENTS:
The Blue Lion, Hardwick.
The Red Lion, Toft.
The Three Horseshoes, Comberton.
The Grape Vine, Comberton.

Walk 35   WINWICK AND OLD WESTON   8m (13km)

Maps: OS Sheets Landranger 142; Pathfinder 939 and 959.
A long walk past two historic churches.
Start: At 105807, All Saints' Church, Winwick.

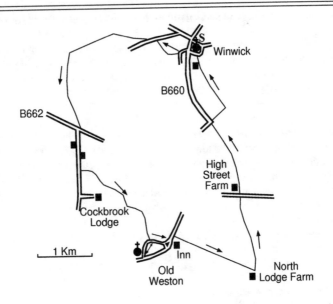

Take the small road opposite **All Saints' Church**, bearing left and, at the left-hand corner, take the track straight ahead. Go through an orchard, then, at the field, turn right and follow the field edge to reach a tarmac road. Cross this, then cross a field diagonally, heading towards the windsock, and then maintaining direction along the field edge and going around the corner to a field gate. Go through and turn left to walk westwards. You are now walking along the county boundary between Cambridgeshire and Northamptonshire. Follow the boundary for about 1,000 yards, then turn left, following an uneven and overgrown path for a further 1,000 yards to reach a main road (the B662). Cross, with care, and walk down the lane opposite, signed 'Cockbrook

Lane'. Walk past a farm, on your right, then another on the left to reach Cock Brook and a public footpath sign, on the left. Follow the path beside the brook, taking care to keep to the path at Cockbrook Lodge where the river bends several times; and as you pass a small orchard where the field edge continues ahead, but the brook, footpath (and footpath signpost) veer to the right. On reaching a lane turn right for about 200 yards to reach **St Swithin's Church, Old Weston**. The route does not visit the church, turning left along the lane, then left again at the main road (the B660) to reach the village.

After about 200 yards, just beyond the inn, cross the road, with care, and turn right along a signed footpath. Follow the path through the trees, then straight across a field. Now walk alongside the edge of the next field until you are level with North Lodge Farm. Now take an obvious path diagonally across the same field to reach a road. Keep to the right of High Street Farm, cross the road and take the track ahead. Follow this wide gravel track almost to the corner of a road. Pass through the hedge ahead, turn right and follow the path along the field edge to reach a clump of trees, on the left, and a path joining from the right. Walk around the trees and continue along the path from the other side. Follow this path, then track, to go through a farm. Walk along the farm drive and turn left at the end to reach the church.

POINTS OF INTEREST:

All Saints' Church, Winwick – The church, with a tower with a broach spire, was built in the 13th and 14th centuries. It has lovely stained glass windows, all of which were restored in the 19th century.

St Swithin's Church, Old Weston – The earliest part of the church dates from the 1200s, though the church is thought not to have been finished until the 13th or 14th century. The top of the tower is quite unusual due to the two (as opposed to just one) horizontal projections from the walls. Inside, there are several interesting paintings.

REFRESHMENTS:
The Swan Inn, Old Weston.

Walks 36 & 37

THE RIPTONS

8m (13km)
or 10½m (17km)

Maps: OS Sheets Landranger 142; Pathfinder 960 and 940.
Scenic countryside walks passing several fine churches.
Start: At 231780, St Andrew's Church, Abbots Ripton.

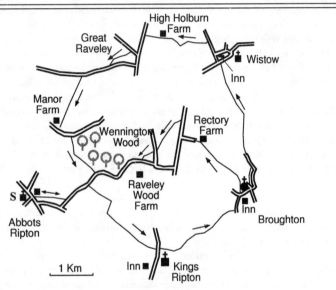

From the church head south to the Three Horseshoes Inn and follow the lane beside it. Go around the slight left bend, then, almost immediately, opposite the lamppost, go through a small gate and follow a signed path across a field. Cross a track, go through a small wood/chicken pen, around a field and across another field to reach a lane. Turn left, follow the lane past the buildings, and take the next track to the right, following it for just over 500 yards to reach an arrowed path on the right. Follow the path around the field edge to the left to reach a river. Turn left along the riverbank to reach a road, crossing a shrubby area and several fields, stiles and bridges. If the path becomes unclear, simply walk with the river on your right. The walk crosses the road and continues along the riverbank, but turn right if you wish to visit St Peter's Church, Kings Ripton. After following the riverbank for about 2 miles you will reach a road. Turn left into **Broughton**, soon reaching All Saints Church and the inn.

The short walk takes the footpath to the left of the church, going through the churchyard and a garden. Go through two fields, then diagonally across another (follow the arrow), heading towards the taller trees next to a gap in a hedge. Follow the waymarked path to Rectory Farm, walk down the farm track and turn right along the road. At the corner at the bottom of a dip, turn left along a footpath beside a drain, following it to a road. Cross and follow the path opposite towards Raveley Wood Farm to reach a track junction. Turn right towards **Wennington Wood**. Follow the signed footpath beside the edge of the wood to reach a signed track on the left, heading away from the wood. The longer route is rejoined here.

The longer walk takes the lane heading north. At its end, cross a stile on the right and cross a field to another stile. Cross and maintain direction to reach a sandy lane. Turn left and at the end, follow the shaded path then the path ahead along the field edges (as waymarked) to reach a drain. Bear left along a field edge, then cross the next field heading towards the right of a tall tree. Follow the path to reach a road in Wistow. Turn right to reach St John the Baptist's Church, then retrace your steps to Harris Lane. Follow the lane for about 500 yards to reach a signed path on the left. Follow the path downhill, then uphill to a road at High Holburn Farm. Turn left, then right into Great Raveley. Go along the road to reach a signed track on the left, following it past farm buildings and on to a bridge beside a wooded area. Cross, immediately duck into the wooded area and follow a drain into a field. Go around to the left and, at a between-fields bridge and hedge, turn right along the field edge to a gravel track. Turn right to reach a barn. From the far corner of the barn follow the obvious path across the field to the far hedge. Turn slightly left along a path to reach a road at Manor Farm, Wennington. Turn left to reach a signed track, on the right, along the edge of Wennington Wood. Follow the track around the wood to the far corner, rejoining the short walk at a path junction.

Follow the track to reach the outward route, retracing your steps back to the Abbots Ripton and the start.

POINTS OF INTEREST:

Broughton – This small, pleasant village has many lovely old houses including Mill House (on your left as you walk into the village) which dates back to 1897.

Wennington Wood – The wood is a designated as a conservation area, providing a vital habitat for native wildlife.

REFRESHMENTS:

The Three Horseshoes, Abbots Ripton.
The Unicorn, Kings Ripton.
The Crown, Broughton.

St Ives 8m (13km)

Maps: OS Sheets Landranger 153 and 142; Pathfinder 960 and 940.

A linear walk through fine fenland country.

Start: At 314712, All Saints' Church, St Ives.

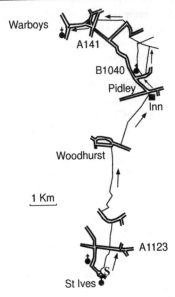

From **All Saints Church**, cross the street/square and turn left. Once in Crown Street, turn right along Crown Place (between Woolworths and the Post Office), then, with a slight left-hand turn, go down Crown Walk, continuing beside a park (on your right). At the end of the park, turn left, then right, and walk ahead into Parkway. At its end, turn right, then left into St Audrey Close. At its end, cross the A1123, with care, and follow the signed path opposite. Go through an orchard and then along a tarmac path for about $\frac{1}{2}$ mile to reach Marley Road. Turn left and continue until you are between Waveney Way and Constable Road, on your left. There are two signed paths to your right: take the path to the left along the right-hand side of a field. Continue along the signed path going around the inside of the top right-hand corners of several fields until, just past the farm buildings, you reach an obvious path across a field. Take this, following it northwards, finally going through a shaded area and up a grassy track to reach a lane. Go ahead, along the lane, into Woodhurst. The main street and **St John's Church** are on your left, beyond the duckpond.

Leave Woodhurst eastwards along the main village road and, after about 400 yards, take the signed path to the left. Follow this path to Pidley, taking care, when you join a grassy track, to cross the bridge to your right and then, at the base of the field, to take a slight left-hand wiggle to reach the next bridge. Take care, too, right at the end of the walk, following the field edge on your right through the raspberry orchard and to the right of a barn. Walk to the main road (the B1040) and bear left along the pavement for $^1/_2$ mile to reach **All Saints' Church**. Go back along the road and take the first road on the left, following it for $^1/_2$ mile, passing a path on the right, to reach one on the left (the sign here may be hidden by trees). Follow the path along a field edge and through an orchard to a small, well-hidden bridge in the bottom corner of the field. Cross and turn left to the end of the field. Turn right along the field edge to reach an overgrown track. Turn left and follow the track up the left-hand field edge to reach another track. Turn left to reach a track junction. Turn right, then take the left-hand fork, keeping left to reach an obvious path. Follow this path into Warboys. At the main road (the A141), turn left, then right continuing for almost a mile up the High Street to reach the Clocktower/Market Place, from where buses leave for St Ives approximately two-hourly on weekdays and four-hourly at weekends.

POINTS OF INTEREST:

All Saints Church, St Ives – In a beautiful situation right beside the river this large, 15th-century church has a very impressive steeple.

St John the Baptist's Church, Woodhurst – This church has work from Norman right up to Victorian times, and has a rather unusual, weather-boarded bell turret.

All Saints Church, Pidley – Built in 1864 with a tower and broach spire.

St Mary Magdalene's Church, Warboys – This is a very grand looking church with a high and impressive tower. Note the interesting door-knocker to the chancel consisting of a lion's head and two fighting dragons.

REFRESHMENTS:

The Mad Cat, Pidley.

The White Hart, Warboys.

There is also a good choice in St Ives.

Walk 39   CHEVELEY   8m (13km)

Maps: OS Sheets Landranger 154; Pathfinder 983 and 1005.

The countryside and stud farms of Newmarket.

Start: At 684609, the Church of St Mary and the Holy Host of Heaven, Cheveley.

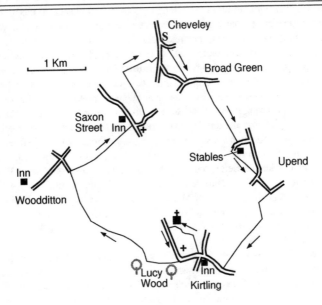

From the **Church of St Mary and the Holy Host of Heaven** in Cheveley, go southwards down the road to reach a small triangular green and a signed footpath. Follow the path through a stud farm, keeping in a relatively straight line to reach a road at Broad Green. Turn left and, after about 500 yards, at a slight bend, take the signed footpath on the right. Walk down the drive and past the house, then go through the stud farm, following the small arrows, but roughly maintaining direction. After almost a mile, where the path ends at a small lane, turn right towards the houses. Go around the back of the houses and the tennis court to join a path heading eastwards. Follow this, but just before reaching a set of stables, turn right along a concrete road. Take the path on the left at the end of the buildings and follow this to the road at Upend. Turn right, and then take the next road on the left, following it for about 500 yards, to the corner, and then taking the track, on the right, for Kirtling. Follow the track to a corner, cross a stile, and go diagonally across the field beyond. Cross three bridges and, beyond the third, turn right along a signed path to reach a road. Turn right to reach the centre of Kirtling. Just after the inn, turn right along a footpath, following it across two fields, around **Kirtling Tower**, and then around another field to reach **All Saints' Church**.

Go through the graveyard to reach a lane and continue to a road. Turn left, passing the **Church of Our Lady Immaculate and St Philip** to reach a footpath on the right, at corner of the road. Follow the path to a junction and turn right. Now walk beside Lucy Wood, almost to its end, to reach a wooden bridge. Turn right and follow a track away from the wood and the bridge. Maintain direction along the track for about $1^1/_2$ miles to reach a signed path on the right (after having been through the wood). Follow this path eastwards to Saxon Street, passing a small row of houses to reach the main village road. Turn right, then take the next road on the left, passing the **Methodist Church**. Follow the road around a corner, then take the signed path on the left, following it through a stud farm to reach the buildings at the far end. Go through a gate on to a path, turn right to follow the path to reach a road in Cheveley. Turn left and follow the road for about 500 yards to return to the church.

POINTS OF INTEREST:

Church of St Mary and the Holy Host of Heaven, Cheveley – This flint and rubble church dates from the early 14th century. The tower, a very imposing structure, is square at the base and octagonal above.

All Saints' Church, Kirtling – The church is mainly Perpendicular in style but does have a very fine Norman doorway. It also houses some splendid monuments, mainly of members of the North family.

Kirtling Tower – This was actually the gatehouse of a mansion. The tower dates from 1530 and is of a style typical of that time – a cross between the medieval and the Renaissance. The mansion was originally the home of the North family.

Church of Our Lady Immaculate and St Philip, Kirtling – This small flint church with a bellcote was built in 1877.

Methodist Church – A small, towerless, Victorian brick-built church.

REFRESHMENTS:
The Red Lion, Cheveley.
The Queens Head, Kirtling.
The Reindeer Inn, Saxon Street.

Walk 40 FULBOURN 8m (13km)

Maps: OS Sheets Landranger 154; Pathfinder 1004.
A very pleasant, but quite long, walk from Fulbourn.
Start: At 520563, St Vigor's Church, Fulbourn.

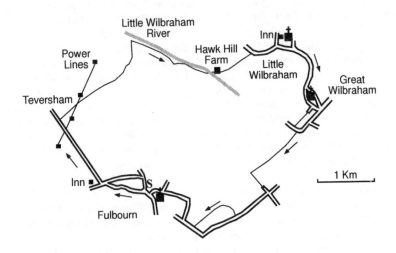

From **St Vigor's Church** in the centre of Fulbourn, take the road heading east beside the store and the butchers, following it for $\frac{1}{2}$ mile through the town to reach the inn. Turn right along the road to Teversham, following it for almost a mile to reach the electricity pylons on the outskirts of the village. Here, take the public footpath on the right, following this lovely path for just over 1 mile to the Little Wilbraham River. Bear right to follow the waymarked Harcamlow Way towards the Wilbrahams. After a mile, at Hawk Mill Farm, turn left along a track into Little Wilbraham.

In Little Wilbraham, maintain direction along the road to reach **St John the Evangelist's Church**. Continue along the road for a further mile into Great Wilbraham. Go past **St Nicholas' Church**, then take the first turning right (Tols Way), and continue along a path to reach a road. Turn left and walk to the left-hand corner. Here, take the path on the right, signed for Fulbourn and Flean Dyke. Follow the path for just over a mile to reach a track. Turn left, and then take the first right along another track. Follow the track to reach a signed path for Fulbourn on the right. Take this path, following it around the edge of a field, and then south-westwards to reach a lane, passing the **Cambridgeshire Green Belt Project Nature Reserve**. At the lane, turn right then take the next turning right and follow this lane/bridleway past the **Fulbourn Educational Nature Reserve** and into Fulbourn. On reaching a road, turn left to return to the start.

POINTS OF INTEREST:

St Vigor's Church, Fulbourn – The church was built in the 13th and 14th centuries, the tower and most of the north facing parts being earlier, while the southern parts were completed later. The interior of the church houses many interesting decorations, including several fine brasses.

St John the Evangelist's Church, Little Wilbraham – Built in the Early English architectural style in the 14th century, though the chancel was rebuilt in 1850.

St Nicholas' Church, Great Wilbraham – This Early English style church is thought to have replaced an earlier Norman building and includes some interesting architectural features.

Cambridgeshire Green Belt Project Nature Reserve, Fulbourn – Developed as a 'green area' close to Cambridge, this Nature Reserve has many different habitats. Plants include bramble, cowslips and oxlips, while animals include field mice and moles.

Fulbourn Educational Nature Reserve, Fulbourn – The Nature Reserve has a mixture of habitats and includes a large number of wetland species (at least in comparison to typical Cambridgeshire country). Indeed, the name Fulbourn is derived from the words 'fowl' and 'burn'. The birdlife in the Reserve includes coots, moorhens and swans. The Reserve also holds numerous dryland species including cowslips and bee-orchids amongst the flowers, and rabbits and moles amongst the animals.

REFRESHMENTS:

The Five Bells, Fulbourn.
The Baker's Arms, Fulbourn.
The Hole in the Wall, Little Wilbraham.
The Carpenter's Arms, Great Wilbraham.

Walk 41   DRY DRAYTON   8m (13km)

Maps: OS Sheets Landranger 154; Pathfinder 981.

A long walk passing some historic churches and woodland.

Start: At 380620, the Church of St Peter and St Paul, Dry Drayton.

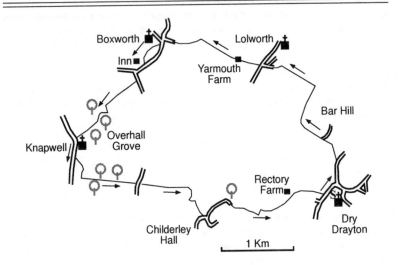

From the **Church of St Peter and St Paul**, walk 100 yards along the road towards Hardwick, then turn right along the High Street. At the end, take the bridleway to Bar Hill. Cross the first footbridge on then left, then walk past a large, scenic duck pond and go through an orchard. Now follow the path parallel to the road and, having walked around the edge of the houses for about a mile, take the signed footpath on the left, following it across fields, bearing slightly left at the end to reach a lane (Cuckoo Lane) at Lolworth. Go past a cottage, on your right, then take the lane to the right to visit **All Saints' Church**. Return to Cuckoo Lane and turn right to continue the walk. At the main road, cross and walk down the lane into Yarmouth Farm. Walk through the farm, bear slightly right and follow the grassy track ahead. Follow the track around to the left, and then the right to reach a lane. Walk down the lane to reach a road in Boxworth. Turn left, then take the next road on your right (Church Lane) to **St Peter's Church**. Walk through the graveyard then cross the end of the lane into a field. Walk straight across the field towards a house, then, at a gate, turn left to the small gate under the telegraph poles. Go through to a road and turn right to reach the inn. Take the road opposite the inn (Battle Gate Road) and, after about 200 yards, around the bend, take the very wide path on the right. Follow the path, crossing a track, to reach the woods. Go over the stile to your left, and cross the field beyond to another wood. Turn right and follow a path along the edge of the wood and, at the bottom of the field, turn left to view **Overhall Grove**, or continue ahead for the walk to **All Saints' Church**. Walk down the lane from the church to reach a road and turn left into Knapwell. After about 200 yards, opposite another path, take the path on the left, following it between gardens, then diagonally across a field. Turn right beside the next field to reach a byway running through the trees. Turn left and follow the byway for just over a mile, crossing the end of a road. At the end, turn right along a track, following it through a chicken farm to a lane. Turn left, away from **Childerley Hall**, following the lane into a clump of trees. At the lane end, take the bridleway ahead, following it beside fields, then go left, through a hedge, and across another field. At the junction in the centre of the field, turn left to reach a track at Rectory Farm. Take the footpath ahead across a field and down an alley to a road. Turn left to regain the start.

POINTS OF INTEREST:

St Peter and St Paul's Church, Dry Drayton – The most noticeable part of this mainly 14th-century church is its tall chancel, which dates from the mid-19th century.
All Saints Church, Lolworth – Though the chancel windows are slightly later, the frieze of bellflowers and flowers strung along a tendril dates the church to 1320.
St Peter's Church, Boxworth – Built of pebble rubble, the church dates mainly from the 14th century, though the north wall may be Norman.
Overhall Grove – The Grove may be the largest surviving elm wood in Britain, and is home to variety of wildlife, including oxlips, bluebells, many species of fungi, woodpeckers, tree creepers and badgers. Originally the Grove was the site of Over Hall Manor, itself built over prehistoric earthworks in 1283 by William de Bokesworth. Unfortunately the manor and estate gradually fell into decay and the woodland took over. Part of the woodland – the Red Well – is thought to date from the 13th century.
All Saints' Church, Knapwell – This small church dates mainly from 1866, but the tower is Perpendicular in style. The church also has an unusual gabled doorway.
Childerley Hall, Childerley – This 16th-century Hall has been described as one of the best seats in the area. At one time it was much larger.

REFRESHMENTS:
The Golden Ball, Boxworth.

Walk 42   CROXTON   8m (13km)

Maps: OS Sheets Landranger 153; Pathfinder 981 and 1003.
A pleasant walk including a fine park.
Start: At 252592, St James' Church, Croxton.

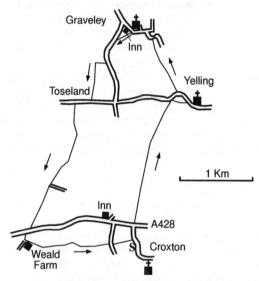

From **St James' Church, Croxton**, near **Croxton Park**, follow the road (High Street) westwards to Croxton village, walking through the village to reach the A428. Turn right, then cross, with care, and take the path on your left (almost opposite where you emerged from the village). Follow this path beside a field and across a bridge. Go straight across the next two fields, then along the edges of several more to reach, after about 2 miles, the corner of a road, opposite the Baptist Church in Yelling. Turn right along a footpath, following it beside a field, then down the next field and across a stream. Now go left, along a bank, to reach a road. Here, turn right, uphill, for 200 yards to reach the **Church of the Holy Cross**, or left to continue the walk. Follow the road through the village for almost 500 yards to reach a bridleway on your right (the bridleway is the second path from the church). Follow the bridleway ahead (as indicated) then round the bottom of a field to reach a lane. Turn left and follow the lane to a road. Turn left into Graveley.

Follow the road, passing **St Botolph's Church** (along a minor road on the right) to reach a three-way road junction and the Market Place. Turn left along a minor road, and then take the public footpath on the right (along the verge not the track). Follow the path around to the right, behind the gardens, and across a field to reach a road. Here turn left, then take the path, on the right, after the bend, marked by white-topped posts. Follow this path to the end of the field, then turn left along the field edge. Continue along the edges of several fields to reach **St Michael's Church** and the road (50 yards further on) at Toseland. Turn right and walk to the slight bend, then take the first track on the left (signed as a bridleway). Follow this wide, grassy track through a small wood and along the edges of several fields to reach a track. Continue ahead, along the track, to reach the A428. Cross, with care, and bear slightly right to take the track to Weald Farm. Follow the path in front of the house, keeping ahead to the end of the concrete road, crossing a stile and walking beside a field. Go through a patch of trees and undergrowth, then walk along the edge of a field to reach a track. Follow the track to reach a road. Turn left, then, soon, take the path on the right (it is almost opposite the path on which you reached the road), and follow it across a (bull's) field to reach Croxton High Street. Turn right to return to the church.

POINTS OF INTEREST:

St James' Church, Croxton – Built in the late 13th century, the church was originally in the old village of Croxton, but is some distance from the present village.

Croxton Park – Built by Edward Leeds in 1803 (his tomb is in St James' Church) this Georgian red-brick house includes many of the typical decorations of the period.

Church of the Holy Cross, Yelling – Built of brown cobbles, this church dates from the 12th to the 14th centuries, the tower being the newest part. Originally there was also a spire.

St Botolph's Church, Graveley – This small Perpendicular church was built in the 14th century, but has been much restored and renewed.

St Michael's Church, Toseland – The church was designed by Arthur Bloomfield and built in 1873, but in a Norman architectural style.

REFRESHMENTS:

The Three Horseshoes, Graveley.

The Cross Keys, Croxton (on the A428).

WHITTLESEY

Maps: OS Sheets Landranger 142; Pathfinder 919.
A combination of the countryside and industry.
Start: At 271971, the Market Place, Whittlesey.

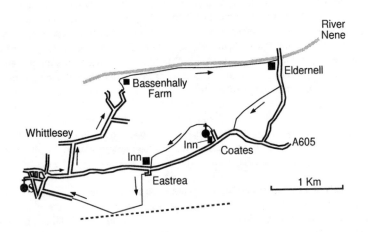

From the **Market Place** in the centre of Whittlesey, take the road going eastwards, following it to its end. Turn left to reach a roundabout. Take the A605, the road to March, walking beside it, with care, for about 500 yards, then turning up Coronation Avenue, on your left. Walk to the end of the avenue, then turn right along Dry Bread Road, passing the Straw Bear Inn and going around to the left to leave the houses. Continue along the road, passing a single house, on the right. Follow the road to the left, then to the right, then take the footpath on the left signed as part of the Nene Way. Follow this grassy track around a Conservation Area and then up on to an embankment. Once on the embankment, follow the Nene Way for just over 2 miles to reach a minor road at Eldernell. Turn right along the road for about 500 yards to reach a track on the right. Take this track and, at its end, follow the path ahead towards the church. Follow the path as it bends around to the left to reach a track. Turn left to reach the A605 at Coates. Turn right and follow the main road, with care, for about 500 yards to reach the green, on your right. Cross this to reach **Holy Trinity Church**.

Facing the church, turn right along the road outside the church and, at its end, take the public byway to the left, following it to Eastrea, finishing by following a minor road to the A605. Cross, with care, and take the track opposite, beside the inn. Follow the path around to the right, then, after about 200 yards, take the track on the left. Follow the track as it bears right beside the railway, continuing along it towards Whittlesey, passing the **Lattersley Local Nature Reserve** along the way and keeping ahead as the track turns into New Road. At the end of the road, turn left, then, very soon, right along Hardy's Lane. At the end of the lane, turn right to reach **St Mary's Church**. Continue along the road, or walk beside the Royal Mail building, to return to the Market Place.

POINTS OF INTEREST:

Market Place, Whittesley – The Market Place, with its Butter Cross, marks the centre of the town and is surrounded by many fine Georgian buildings. Note particularly the Post Office House.

Holy Trinity Church, Coates – Built of yellow brick, this church dates from 1840 but is Norman in style rather than Victorian.

Lattersley Local Nature Reserve – Once a refuse tip, the Reserve has recently been developed and is gradually becoming home to a variety of wildlife, including cowslips, cow parsley and brambles, rabbits, shrews and voles, and kestrels.

St Mary's Church, Whittlesey – The church is mainly in the Decorated and Perpendicular English Gothic styles of architecture, although the tower seems to have been a later addition. The church is considered by some to have one of the most splendid spires in Cambridgeshire.

REFRESHMENTS:

The Straw Bear, Whittlesey.
The Vine Inn, Coates.
The Carpenter's Arms, Coates.
The Nags Head, Eastrea.
There are also numerous possibilities in Whittlesey.

Walk 44   **KIMBOLTON**   8m (13km)

Maps: OS Sheets Landranger 153; Pathfinder 980.
Typical Cambridgeshire Countryside, Villages and Churches.
Start: At 099679, St Andrew's Church, Kimbolton.

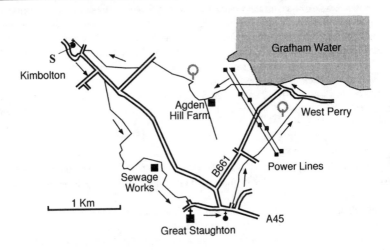

From **St Andrew's Church, Kimbolton** walk down the High Street towards **Kimbolton Castle**, then continue around the corner into Stonely. Go past the B660 to Bedford and take the next path on the right, following it to a track. Continue along the track to its end, then turn right beside a dyke. On reaching a brook (the River Kym) turn left beside it for just under a mile to reach a track on the left. Follow this track to its end and turn left. Follow the track around the far side of the sewage works to rejoin the River Kym and turn left. After 500 yards, cross the river and keep ahead along a track. Now take the next track on the left, following it for about a mile. Now turn left, and then right around the grounds of Place House (a fine Jacobean mansion) to reach a road opposite **St Andrew's Church, Great Staughton**. Turn left to reach the A45. Turn right, with care, passing the **Village Cross** to reach the deconsecrated church. Take the road opposite the church and continue along Moory Croft Close (a No Through Road) and the footpath at its end. Maintain direction across, and beside several fields to reach a road. Turn right, but soon turn left along a signed path. Follow this waymarked path beside fields to reach an inn car park in West Perry.

Walk to the road and turn left, following the road to the car park for the **Grafham Water Nature Reserve**. Go through the car park to the Reserve and walk through it to reach a cycle path. Turn right to reach the point where a bridleway is signed ahead, and cyclists are asked to turn right. Follow the bridleway around several fields and under the electricity wires to reach Agden Hill Farm. Go past the front of the house, then turn right, as if following the house front, to go along a path. Follow the right-hand edges of three fields to the corner of a wood. Turn left beside the wood, then, after almost 300 yards, at the next corner of the wood, turn left and follow a signed bridleway to a road. Turn left for about 200 yards to reach a footpath on the right. Follow this obvious path across two fields towards the main road. Before reaching the road, turn right along another obvious path, crossing two more fields to reach a lane. Turn right past the houses to reach another obvious path on the left. Cross a field to reach the cemetery. Turn left, cross a bridge and keep to the left to reach the church.

POINTS OF INTEREST:

St Andrew's Church, Kimbolton – In a variety of styles and suffering many renovations, but has a fine tower and spire, both dating from the 14th century.

Kimbolton Castle – Built on the site of the original medieval castle, the Castle was built in the 17th century and then extensively remodelled by Vanbrugh (the designer of both Blenheim Palace and Castle Howard). Although not as grand or architecturally ornate, the Castle is definitely worth a look, as too are its grounds.

St Andrew's Church, Great Staughton – The church has an ostentatious Perpendicular tower and houses a number of very interesting monuments and paintings.

Village Cross, Great Staughton – Situated outside Dial House, Great Staughton's village cross is, in fact, a sundial and dates from 1637.

Grafham Water Nature Reserve – Created in the mid-1960s as a reservoir, Grafham Water is now a Site of Specific Scientific Interest for its waterbirds. The entire west side of the reservoir has been designated a Nature Reserve. The wildlife includes nightingales, tufted ducks, herons and great-crested grebes.

REFRESHMENTS:

The Saddle, Kimbolton.
The Tavern, Great Staughton (on the A45/B661 crossroads).
The Tickled Trout, West Perry.
The New Sun Inn, Kimbolton.
The Wheatsheaf, West Perry.
The White Hart Inn, Great Staughton.

Walk 45   SPALDWICK   8m (13km)

Maps: OS Sheets Landranger 153; Pathfinder 959 and 980.
A pleasant walk including the edge of Grafham Water.
Start: At 128728, St James' Church, Spaldwick.

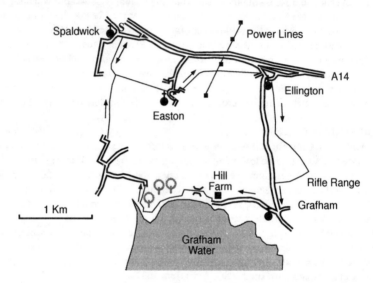

From **St James' Church, Spaldwick**, head towards the A14, and take the next road on the right. Follow this road for almost a mile, then take the public byway on the left, following it for just over a mile to reach a lane. Walk down the lane to reach **St Peter's Church, Easton**. From the church, continue eastwards to reach a crossroads. Turn left to reach the main road. Turn right, then left (so continuing to walk straight ahead), to follow a lane. Follow the lane left, then right to reach a footpath on the left at the end of a hedge. Follow this path/track around the edges of several fields and under the electricity wires towards Ellington. If in doubt you should be walking eastwards and quite close to the main road (the A14), passing between the two electricity pylons which are nearest to the road. At the end of the track, go through a farm on to a road and turn right to reach the centre of Ellington and **All Saints' Church**.

Go through the churchyard to reach a lane and turn left to reach its end. Take the footpath ahead, following it along the edges of, and directly across, several fields to reach a concrete track. Cross the track and go across the field beyond, following an obvious path to reach a bridleway on the other side of a brook. You are now on a rifle range and should take care. If red flags are flying the range should be avoided. Turn right and follow the bridleway to a road. Turn left and follow the road for about $\frac{1}{2}$ mile to reach a crossroads. Turn right to reach **All Saints' Church, Grafham**.

Continue along the road until it ends just past Hill Farm. Walk through the car park then take the signed bridleway, following it uphill slightly until and going under a bridge. Beyond the bridge, take the first path on the left to join the bridleway running across the top of the bridge. Follow this bridleway for just over a mile as it returns almost to the side of the lake and passes through a small wood. Immediately before coming out of the wood (or immediately after if the path is overgrown) take the path on the right, following it up the side of the wood to reach a track. Follow the track ahead, then turn left with it and walk to a road. Turn right, then take the next track on the left. Follow this track around to the right, then, as it veers to the left, take the obvious bridleway directly across the fields towards Spaldwick. Follow the bridleway to reach a track and turn right to follow the track into the village. On reaching a road, turn left to return to the church.

POINTS OF INTEREST:

St James' Church, Spaldwick – The church is a mixture of styles from Norman to Perpendicular English Gothic. It has a very interesting tall 14th-century tower.

St Peter's Church, Easton – This church is mainly in the Perpendicular style, and has a particularly fine tower.

All Saints' Church, Ellington – This church was apparently built completely independently of its very elegant west tower.

All Saints' Church, Grafham – This small church originally dates from the 13th century, but appears to have had many additions at later dates.

REFRESHMENTS:

The George, Spaldwick.
The Mermaid, Ellington.
The Montagu Arms, Grafham.

Walk 46   CROYDON $8\frac{1}{2}$m ($13\frac{1}{2}$km)

Maps: OS Sheets Landranger 153; Pathfinder 1003 and 1026.

A fine walk with a variety of points of interest.

Start: At 312492, Clopton Close, Croydon.

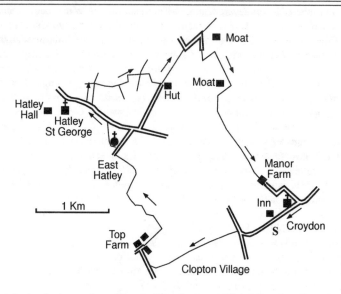

Start at the lay-by/car park on Clopton Close in the middle of Croydon. From it, walk westwards, uphill, along the road to reach a road junction. Cross the road and go straight ahead through the farm, following the bridleway. Continue along the bridleway for just over a mile, passing through **Clopton Village**, to reach a track. Turn right and walk to Top Farm. Walk straight through the farm to reach a gravel track behind the first lot of barns. Turn right and follow the track, passing the house and continuing along the grassy track ahead. After about 500 yards, follow the track around to the left and along field edges, passing a small wood. Continue past a slight kink in the track through a small clump of trees to reach a track junction, just over a stream/dyke. Turn right, following the path as it bears left to reach a small alley at East Hatley. Follow the alley to a road and turn right. After about 50 yards, turn left along a signed footpath to reach **St Denis' Church** and the **St Denis' Church Nature Reserve**. Walk through the graveyard and turn right along a track, following it to a road. Turn left and follow the road for a mile or so into Hatley St George (winner of the 'Best Kept Village in Cambridgeshire' Award in 1990), continuing to **St George's Church** and **Hatley Hall**. Retrace your steps for about 500 yards towards the village and take the signed bridleway on the left. Follow the track to a bridge, cross and turn right to follow a path along the edges of several fields, keeping ahead wherever there is a choice. When you reach a track and are opposite a hut, turn left, following the track for just under a mile to where it turns sharply right. Turn with the track, following it around further sharp bends to the left and then right past an ancient moat. Turn right and left again, then follow the main track down to Manor Farm. Be careful, in several places, where the track is not quite straight ahead: it should still be followed. At the farm, walk down the drive to reach **All Saints' Church** and the main village road in Croydon. Turn right to reach the start.

POINTS OF INTEREST:

Clopton Village – This was the site of a Roman settlement, then more recently the site of an Anglo-Saxon village. At its height the village is thought to have included 2 manors, 19 houses, numerous farms and fields and a population of 500-600. The village was badly effected by Black Death in the mid-14th century, was dying by 1480 and was extinct by 1561. The site is now a scheduled monument.

St Denis' Church, East Hatley – Now disused and abandoned, very little except the outer shell of this 14th-century church remains, yet with its covering of ivy the building still has a lot of character.

St Denis' Church Nature Reserve – Since the decline and abandonment of the church this area of land has been left to run wild and turned into a local Nature Reserve. The Reserve is home to numerous species including cowslips and orchids, and a variety of insects and rodents.

St George's Church, Hatley St George – The church was originally in Perpendicular style, but has since been much rebuilt. Most noticeably the tower was rebuilt in 1625 and the chancel in 1878.

Hatley Hall, Hatley St George – This large brick house was originally built in the 17th century, but was altered and added to in the 18th century.

All Saints' Church, Croydon – This small church dates from the 14th century and considering its small size is architecturally quite ornate.

REFRESHMENTS:
The Queen Adelaide, Croydon.

Walk 47　　　　　　　OVER　　　　　　　9m (14km)

Maps: OS Sheets Landranger 154 and 153; Pathfinder 960 and 981.

A walk along the Great Ouse River visiting several fine churches.
Start: At 372708, St Mary's Church, Over.

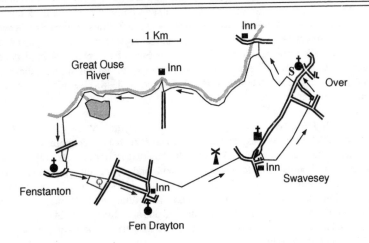

From **St Mary's Church**, walk southwards along the main road to reach Longholme Lane and a signed track for Overcote. Follow the track around to the left, then straight ahead to reach an embankment. Turn right along the top of the embankment, following it for about $1/2$ mile to reach a small bridge to your left. Cross and continue along the embankment, which becomes the riverside path beside the **Great Ouse River**. After almost 2 miles, the path gradually moves away from the river and the embankment stops: maintain direction, heading for a gate on to a sandy track. Turn right and follow the track towards the river (and the inn on the other side). At the river, turn left and walk beside it, at first on a bridleway, then on a footpath. Follow the footpath under an old railway bridge and into a field. Walk halfway along the field edge, then turn left along a broad, signed path. At a track, do a slight right-hand wiggle, then continue ahead to reach the playing fields. Walk around to the left to reach **St Peter and St Paul's Church, Fenstanton**. Retrace your steps and take the signed path to the right. Follow this path and then a track across fields, then take the path to the left of the woods to reach Fen Drayton. Walk along the street and then around the corner to the right, leaving the inn to your left. Continue ahead down a small road to reach **St Mary's Church** on your left. Return to the inn, go straight along its front and continue along this lane for $^{1}/_{2}$ mile. Now turn right along a signed path, crossing a footbridge and follow the well-trodden path through fields. Maintain direction along a signed track, going beneath a windmill to reach the end of Taylors Lane. Go straight ahead to reach the main road in Swavesey, with the inn and village centre about 200 yards to your right, and **St Andrew's Church** about 800 yards ahead. From the church, retrace your steps to reach a small gate to the left, just after the river. Follow the path beyond through a field and across the first bridge to reach a small lane. Turn left and, after 500 yards, take the left-hand fork, signed for Over. Go through fields, over the railway and through an orchard to reach a lane. Cross and maintain direction along the road opposite. Turn left along the first path, following it past the recreation grounds to reach a lane. Continue ahead to the main road and turn right to reach the church.

POINTS OF INTEREST:

St Mary's Church, Over – The church used to belong to Ramsey Abbey and, possibly as a result, is very ornately decorated, both inside and out, with very detailed friezes and gargoyles, pinnacles and battlements.

St Peter and St Paul's Church, Fenstanton – This is a typical country church of the 14th century, the most interesting part of which is its chancel, noted for its height and elegant windows.

St Mary's Church, Fen Drayton – The church is unusual in that it is built of pebble rubble. It probably dates from the 14th century, but may be Saxon.

St Andrew's Church, Swavesey – This large early 14th-century church has an unusually fine exterior, particularly if viewed from the south.

Great Ouse River – The Great Ouse River Valley provides some of the most interesting and attractive countryside in the county. In such an expanse of dry arable land as Cambridgeshire, the river and the water-filled gravel pits provide a rare and valuable habitat for water species – reeds, rushes and marshplants, dragonflies and butterflies, coots, moorhens and swans. In addition to this the river flood meadows provide a permanent grassland habitat, rich in mature trees and wild flower species such as cowslips, crosswort and salad burnet.

REFRESHMENTS:
The Admiral Vernon, Over.
The Three Tuns, Fen Drayton.
The White Horse, Swavesey.

Walk 48   SOHAM   9m (14km)

Maps: OS Sheets Landranger 154; Pathfinder 961, 962 and 982.
A walk with a nice variety of points of interest.
Start: At 594732, St Andrew's Church, Soham.

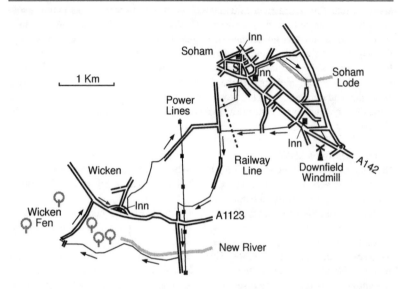

From the church, walk southwards down the High Street to the crossroads. Turn left and, after 100 yards, you will reach two paths on the right. Take the less obvious path on the other side of the house, following it beside the river for almost a mile to reach a concrete bridge. Cross and follow a track straight ahead, to reach a lane. Go straight down the lane to reach a road. Turn left and walk to the corner. Here, take the track straight ahead, following it through fields in the direction of the windmill. On meeting a road, turn left and walk to Windmill Close. Now follow the brown windmill signs to **Downfield Windmill**. Walk back up the road towards Soham and, after about ¹/₂ mile, just beyond the roundabout, take the signed track to your left. Follow the track, then maintain direction along a lane. Cross the railway, with care, into a field and walk with a hedge to your right. At the corner do not leave the field: instead, follow the right-hand hedge to the next corner. There, follow a beautiful, shaded path, staying on it to reach a track just the other side of the electricity lines. Turn left along the track to reach the main road (the A1123). Cross, with care, and follow the track opposite to reach a concrete bridge over New River. Cross and turn right, following the river for $1^1/_2$ miles to reach a small bridge. Cross and walk up the lane past **Wicken Fen** to reach the main road (the A1123) again. Turn right to the centre of Wicken.

Go to the right of the inn and walk down the small road to reach a path to your right. Follow this well-trodden path around the edge of the allotments and then around the edges of, and straight across, several fields, following the waymarkers and maintaining roughly the same direction (heading towards the obvious tower of St Andrew's Church in Soham). The path becomes a track: continue along it to reach a lane. Turn left and walk up the lane for about 500 yards to reach a signed footpath on your right. Take this well-trodden path, crossing stiles, bridges and fields to reach a school playing field. Follow the waymarkers along the edge of the field to your left and then follow a tarmac path to a lane. Turn right, then cross the river and continue up the road ahead. At the top, turn left slightly to reach a footpath along an alley, following it into the churchyard of **St Andrew's Church**.

POINTS OF INTEREST:
Downfield Windmill, Soham – Originally built about 1720, but rebuilt in 1890 and recently restored, Downfield is a good example of a smock-type windmill, though it is slightly unusual as it has an octagonal base.
Wicken Fen – The Fen is a National Nature Reserve owned by the National Trust and is one of the most important wetland habitats in Britain. Surrounded by such a dry and intensely farmed land, the 600 acre wetland (originally part of the Great Fen Levels) provides a vital habitat for numerous plant, insect and mammal species. Marked walks, hides and watchtowers are provided, as is detailed information on the site and its wildlife, with further information and displays on the history of the area. There is an entry fee for the Reserve. Note that the Reserve has only one entrance/exit i.e. you can not walk through it.
St Andrew's Church, Soham – This is a beautiful example of a church built in the Perpendicular style of English Gothic architecture, but with some rather extravagant additions. The chancel is particularly noteworthy, especially its stalls, panelling and stained-glass windows.

REFRESHMENTS:
The Fountain, Soham.
The Red Lion, Soham.
The Cherry Tree, Soham.
The Maids Head, Wicken.

Maps: OS Sheets Landranger 154; Pathfinder 1005.

A fine walk through typical Cambridgeshire countryside and villages.

Start: At 686576, All Saints' Church, Kirtling.

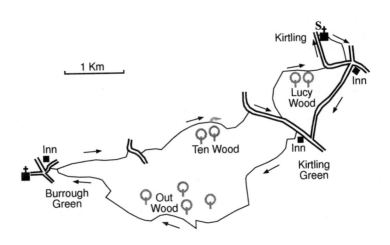

From **All Saints' Church**, walk away from the road, following a signed footpath across fields and around **Kirtling Towers**, eventually reaching the village road again, just before the inn. At the road junction, take the road straight ahead, following it for a mile or so to reach Kirtling Green. At the junction at the top of the village, turn right and, after about 200 yards, take the signed footpath on the left. Follow the path around the reservoir and then beside a dyke. After just over a mile, when a path crosses yours (the second signed path), turn right and follow the obvious path across two fields. Now maintain direction to reach the corner of Out Wood. Follow the edge of the wood to its end then turn left, going slightly back on yourself to reach a stile on the left. Turn directly away from the stile and walk across the field to reach another woodland corner. Now follow the woodland edge again (this is still Out Wood). Follow the edge for about $^1/_2$ mile, then follow the signed path through it. On emerging at the other side, turn right and follow the edge of a field around to the left. Maintain direction through a small cluster of trees to reach a track on your right. Follow this track to the top of the hill, then turn left, following a waymarked path towards Burrough Green. Cross a footbridge and go between two houses to reach the main village street, the inn and **St Augustine's Church**.

Retrace your steps to the footbridge and take the signed path eastwards. Follow the path around the edge of the several fields and small woods, continuing to head eastwards, but finally turning slightly northwards to reach a road. Turn right along the road for about 500 yards to reach a signed footpath on the left. Follow this path eastwards to Ten Wood. Now follow the path around the wood, and then beside it (the path is not too obvious here). At the far edge of the wood you will reach a track: turn right (as waymarked) for about 500 yards, then turn left (again as waymarked) to rejoin the original path. Now follow this path to a road. Turn right for about 500 yards, then take the footpath on the left, turning slightly back on yourself. Follow the path beside Lucy Wood and, at its end, turn left to reach a road. Turn left and walk uphill past the **Church of Our Lady Immaculate and St Philip** to reach the starting church.

POINTS OF INTEREST:

All Saints' Church, Kirtling – The church is mainly Perpendicular in style but does have a very fine Norman doorway. It also houses some splendid monuments, mainly to members of the North family.

Kirtling Tower – This was actually the gatehouse of a mansion. The tower dates from 1530 and is of a style typical of that time – a cross between the medieval and the Renaissance. The mansion was originally the home of the North family.

St Augustine's Church, Burrough Green – Though mainly built in the 14th century, the church shows a very interesting variety and mixture of architectural styles. It houses a number of interesting and unusual monuments, mainly of knights and their ladies.

Church of Our Lady Immaculate and St Philip, Kirtling – This small flint church with a bellcote was built in 1877.

REFRESHMENTS:

The Queens Head, Kirtling.
The Red Lion, Kirtling Green.
The Bull Inn, Burrough Green.

Walk 50   **MELDRETH AND MELBOURN**   9m (14km)

Maps: OS Sheets Landranger 154; Pathfinder 1026.
A pleasant long walk through fine villages.
Start: At 378468, Holy Trinity Church, Meldreth.

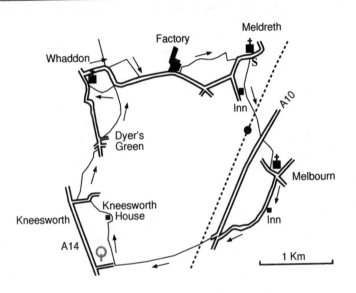

Head down the road opposite **Holy Trinity Church, Meldreth**, to reach Topcliffe
Mill. Immediately before the Mill, turn left along a signed footpath, following it around
the side of a house and then over the river. Go over a stile and walk along the near
edge of the field then continue beside the river passing under the railway and the A10.
On reaching the playing fields, after about a mile, stay beside the river until you have
reached the far side of the fields, then head for the gate/path corner in the middle of
the field edge. Follow the path away from the playing fields – not towards the church,
but towards the road. At the road, turn left to reach **All Saints' Church** and a road
junction. Turn right along the High Street, following it for about a mile to reach the
A10. (At the end of the houses, take the path through a small wood on the left. The
path runs parallel to the road and is much pleasanter to walk along. On leaving the
wood cross the road: the path on the other side is tarmac and easier to follow.) At the

A10, cross, with great care, and take the signed track ahead, following it for just over a mile (going under the railway) to reach a path, on the right, opposite the start of the glass-houses. Follow this path across a field, then beside woodland. Go around **Kneesworth House** and maintain direction to reach a road. Turn left into Kneesworth.

To leave, retrace your steps along Chestnut Lane and take the path on your left, following it for almost a mile, beside fields, to reach Dyer's Green. On meeting a track, turn left, walking ahead, and then around to the right. Take the next track on your right (signed as a footpath), following it through Fountain Farm, then beside a dyke and several fields to reach a road at Whaddon. Do not go on to the road: instead, turn back on yourself slightly and cross the field. Maintain direction until there is a choice of paths: take the right-hand one, following it to a road. Turn right and follow the road around to the right to reach **St Mary's Church, Whaddon**. Continue along the road to the corner. Now take the signed path ahead, following it around to the right to reach a road. Turn left and follow the road for just under a mile, then take the signed footpath, on the left, immediately after the factory. Follow the path over a bridge and across three fields to reach a lane. Turn right, then, soon, left along a path, following it to a road. Now turn left to return to the church, or right to visit the centre of **Meldreth**.

POINTS OF INTEREST:

Holy Trinity Church, Meldreth – Apart from the chancel, which is Norman, this church is predominantly of Perpendicular English Gothic architecture, though some Decorated and Early English architecture can still be seen.

All Saints' Church, Melbourn – This church dates mainly from two eras – the 13th and 16th centuries. Aspects of the tower, nave and aisles, and the chancel are the oldest parts of the church and can still be seen as such despite all the restoration, rebuilding and additions. Melbourn was the winner of the 'Best Kept Village in Cambridgeshire' Award in 1991.

Kneesworth House – Built in 1901, this house is in Neo-Georgian style.

St Mary's Church, Whaddon – This church, built mainly in the Perpendicular style of English Gothic architecture despite its small size, is rather elegant and also quite well decorated architecturally.

Meldreth – The old stocks and whipping post can be found under the chestnut tree on the green in the centre of the village.

REFRESHMENTS:
The British Queen, Meldreth.
The Dolphin, Melbourn.

Walk 51   **RIVER NENE**   9m (14km)

Maps: OS Sheets Landranger 142; Pathfinder 918.
A beautiful walk along the River Nene, returning by steam train.
Start: At 193987, Cathedral Place, Peterborough.

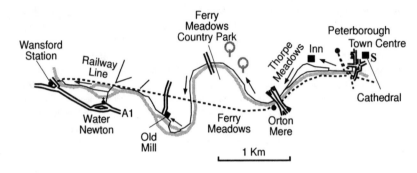

With your back to the Cathedral (*see* Note to Walk 8), facing the Market Place, turn left down Bridgate. Walk through the town, passing the Town Hall, on your left. Cross the dual carriageway, with care, and continue to the sign for Railworld, on the right. Go under the arch and, at the end of the road (on reaching Asda), turn left to reach the River Nene (*see* Note to Walk 8). Keeping on this side of the river, turn right along the riverside path, following this tarmac path under the Iron Bridge (*see* Note to Walk 8) and the railway bridge. Go past Railworld (*see* Note to Walk 8) on the other side of the river, then, at the end of the path, cross the bridge and follow the path beside the Boathouse Inn, keeping the inn to your right.

Continue along the path through **Thorpe Meadows Sculpture Park**. At the end of the Park, continue along the path going under the road bridge and past the lock at Orton Mere. Continue beside the river, passing a golf course and practice area, on the right, and **Ferry Meadows Country Park**, on your left, across the river. After about a mile you will reach a bridge over the river. Do not cross: instead, turn right slightly, then left to maintain direction through a bluebell wood. At any point where the path forks, take the branch on the left to stay close to the river.

At the end of the wood you will reach a road bridge over the river in to the Country Park. Cross the road (but not the river) and take the path ahead, following it beside the river. Go under the railway line, and continue beside the river to reach a footbridge. Cross, walk straight ahead and bear right beside the main part of the river to reach a lock. Turn right and follow a path diagonally across a field to reach a bridge. Recross the smaller arm of the river here, turn left and follow the path around to the front of the Old Mill.

Go up the drive, but, soon, turn left along a path. After about $^1/_2$ mile, at a path junction, take the left-hand path, following it to a small bridge. Cross to regain the riverbank and turn right along it for just over a mile to reach a large bridge on the left. Cross and follow the path ahead to reach the lock at Water Newton. Use the lock to cross the main arm of the river and walk around the very picturesque watermill and 18th-century, lock-keeper's cottage to a road. Turn right and right again to visit the **Church of St Remigius**. Return to the lock, recross the river and turn left beside it. Take this path. Cross a weir by bridge and turn left to reach Wansford. Cross the railway bridge over the river and then cross the road to Wansford station.

To return to Peterborough, take a steam train of the **Nene Valley Railway** to reach Railworld, retracing the outward walk from there.

POINTS OF INTEREST:
Thorpe Meadows Sculpture Park – Situated in a beautiful spot beside the River Nene, the Sculpture Park is a fantastic mix of the beauty of nature and modern art. There are numerous sculptures, all by local artists. The works include Peterborough Arch, Festival Boat, Lagoon, Helios II, Odd Oaks, Endless Omen, Boundaries, and Second Entrance.
Ferry Meadows Country Park, Peterborough – Occupying a risen flood meadow of the River Nene, the Ferry Meadows Country Park is a large and beautiful area of meadowland, but also includes some lovely bluebell woodland. Various leisure activities, including walking, cycling, golf, and a few watersports are available here.
St Remigius' Church, Water Newton – Mainly in the Early English style of architecture, though the chancel suffered some alterations in the 17th century.
Nene Valley Railway – The railway runs for 15 miles from Peterborough to Yarwell Junction, passing through the Ferry Meadows Country Park and the haunted Wansford Tunnel. It is one of the finest steam railways in the country and is the home of the original Thomas the Tank Engine.

REFRESHMENTS:
Peterborough has a variety of refreshments for all tastes and budgets.
The Boathouse Inn, at the entrance to Thorpe Meadows Sculpture Park.

Walk. 52   **MARCH**   9m (14km)

Maps: OS Sheets Landranger 142; Pathfinder 919 and 920.

The flatness and farming of the fens.

Start: At 416964, St Peter's Church, March.

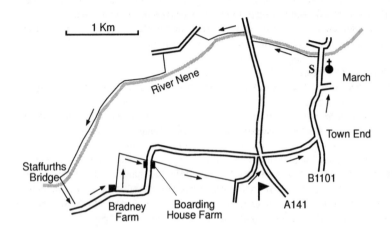

From **St Peter's Church, March**, turn right and walk along the main street, heading towards the War Memorial in the centre of the town. Before reaching the War Memorial, and immediately before crossing the river, turn left along the riverside path. Follow the path past shops and a park, walking beside the **River Nene** to reach the A141. Climb up on to the road, cross the road, with care, and the river, then continue beside the river for a further 3 miles or so to reach Staffurth's Bridge amidst various farm and yard buildings and a campsite, detouring from the river at one point to walk along a road for about 400 yards, then rejoining the river by the permissive path.

Turn left and follow a track to a road. Turn left and follow the road past Bradney Farm. Now take the next turning left, along a public byway, following it straight ahead for about 500 yards. Stay on the byway as it turns sharp right, following it straight ahead for almost 2 miles, crossing a road by Boarding House Farm, to reach track. Follow the track as it becomes a road, then turn left and follow the track to a larger road. Turn right to reach the A47. Cross, with care, and continue along the road opposite to reach Town End, on the outskirts of March. The road you are on reaches the B1101: turn left, then left again to visit the **Church of St Wendreda**.

From the church, return to the main road and turn left to continue into March reaching the starting church after another mile of walking.

POINTS OF INTEREST:

St Peter's Church, March – Built in 1880 by Wyatt, this church is of a typical Cambridgeshire design.

River Nene – The River Nene, as with the other rivers running over the dry and flat countryside of Cambridgeshire, provides a valuable habitat for various water species, including reeds, rushes and waterlilies, dragonflies and butterflies, and numerous waterbirds including coots, moorhens, swans, geese and the occasional kingfisher.

Church of St Wendreda, Town End – Apart from the earlier north arcade and the chancel, which were rebuilt in 1872, this church is predominantly in the Decorated style of English Gothic architecture, though it also has a considerable number of Perpendicular additions. The church also has a very fine timber roof.

REFRESHMENTS:

There is plenty of choice in March.

Walk 53   **LITTLEPORT**   9m (14km)

Maps: OS Sheets Landranger 143; Pathfinder 941 and 961.
A linear walk exploring the flatness and farming of the fens.
Start: At 566869, St George's Church, Littleport.

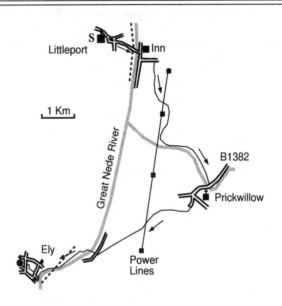

Walk beside **St George's Church, Littleport**, down Church Lane and around to the
left to a crossroads. Go straight ahead to the main street, following it through the town
centre and continuing to the railway line. Cross the railway, with care, and continue
to a road junction. Turn right, then, after 200 yards turn left and follow a road for
about 200 yards to reach a track/path on the right, just after a building. Follow this
track/path beside a dyke, and follow the dyke (on your right) underneath the electricity
wires and around to the right. Now turn right along a loose tarmac road, passing a
storage area, on the left, to reach a road. Turn left and walk on top of an embankment
to reach the main road (the B1382) at Prickwillow. Cross, with care, to reach the
Drainage Engine Museum and **St Peter's Church**. The walk turns right along the
main road to reach the junction of the B1382 and the B1104. Cross diagonally to the
minor road opposite. The road becomes a track: continue along it, following the

106

Hereward Way. Continue along the track to a road. Turn right, and then left, as signed, to reach a bridge over the Great Ouse River. Cross and follow a path around the sides of a car park and through the undergrowth to reach a factory. Go straight up the drive and, at the front entrance, take the signed path on the left. Follow the path beside the car park, then through several fields. After passing under a bridge, keep following the riverside path through a meadow and past a road end to reach the Cutters Inn. Walk in front of the inn, then down its left-hand side towards the car park. Maintain direction along an alley beside the car park and, at the end, walk along Jubilee Terrace (passing Hereward Housing) to reach a road. Turn right, walk to the black signpost on the other side of the road and turn left to walk through a park. At the top of the park, walk along the lane to reach **Ely Cathedral**. You may either enter the Cathedral here and leave by the main entrance, or walk to the right, through the grounds, to reach the main entrance. Now either walk ahead across the green to **Oliver Cromwell's House** and the Tourist Information Office, or go through the gate on the left of the Cathedral to reach the town centre.

There is a bus from Ely to Littleport approximately every other hour on weekdays and every three hours on weekend days. It leaves from Market Street, the main shopping street just to the left of the Cathedral.

POINTS OF INTEREST:

St George's Church, Littleport – A large church, mainly in Perpendicular style. A complete second nave was added to the church in 1857.

St Peter's Church, Prickwillow – The church houses a very fine font, made of white marble and superbly carved and decorated, a gift from Ely Cathedral in 1693.

Drainage Engine Museum, Prickwillow – This Industrial Heritage Centre provides an interesting insight into the drainage and irrigation of the fens. There are numerous engines dating from the turn of the century. On steam days the engines are active.

Ely Cathedral – Set on the Isle of Ely, standing far above the rest of the town, the Cathedral was built from 1081-1189 on the site of an ancient monastery. It is a superb example of Romanesque architecture. Take particular note of the beautiful Octagon which replaced the collapsed Norman tower, the 14th-century Lady Chapel and its carvings, the Prior's Door and the lovely painted ceiling of the Nave.

Oliver Cromwell's House, Ely – This 17th-century house, once the home of Oliver Cromwell, provides an excellent insight into the life of the times.

REFRESHMENTS:
There are numerous possibilities in Littleport and Ely.

Walk 54   ELY – THE BISHOPS WAY   9m (14km)

Maps: OS Sheets Landranger 143; Pathfinder 941.

A famous walk through medieval Ely and its surrounds.

Start: At 540803, Ely Cathedral.

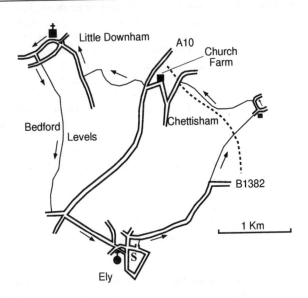

The Bishops Way is a famous walk around the interesting places in the medieval history of Ely and its surrounds. It is very well waymarked at all points.

From the main entrance to **Ely Cathedral**, walk around the Cathedral to the left to reach Sanscrit Gate. Go through the gate into Ely's main shopping street and walk straight ahead along the small passage between Oxfam and New Look to reach the pedestrian precinct. Go straight ahead to reach Newnham Road, following it to its end. Turn right along the B1382, heading towards Prickwillow.

Follow the road for just over a mile to reach a sharp right-hand bend. Now go straight ahead along a lane waymarked as the Bishops Way. Follow the lane over the railway, with care, to reach a building, on your right, and a track, on your left. Take

108

the track to reach a path on the left. Follow the path for about a mile to reach a road. Turn left into Chettisham. At the next road junction, turn right to reach Church Farm. Just before the farm, take the waymarked byway on the left to reach the A10.

Cross, with care, and continue along the waymarked track opposite. Follow the track around to the left, then take the next track on the right, following it to its junction with another track. Turn left to reach a road. Turn right and walk into Little Downham, following the road to reach **St Leonard's Church** (leaving the Bishops Way).

To continue, walk along the road past the church and take the second road on your left. Follow the road to its end, then, returning to the Bishops Way, maintain direction along the Hereward Way. Follow the Hereward Way for almost 2 miles to reach a minor road. Turn left to reach the A10. Cross, with care, and continue along the road opposite for about a mile to reach the B1411 in **Ely**. Go ahead along this road, following it around to the right to reach **Oliver Cromwell's House** and the Tourist Information Office. Now cross the green to return to the Cathedral.

POINTS OF INTEREST:

Ely Cathedral – Set on the Isle of Ely, standing far above the rest of the town, the Cathedral was built from 1081-1189 on the site of an ancient monastery. It is a superb example of Romanesque architecture. Take particular note of the beautiful Octagon which replaced the collapsed Norman tower, the 14th-century Lady Chapel and its carvings, the Prior's Door and the lovely painted ceiling of the Nave.

St Leonard's Church, Little Downham – Built over a long period of time during the 13th century, this church is a gradual mix of Norman and early Gothic architecture. It also has some additions from later dates, such as the porch and the aisle windows.

Ely – Apart from the Cathedral and Cromwell's House, the city has many other very interesting historic buildings, including the Maltings, the Almonry, the Monastic Buildings in the College, the Great Hall and Queens Hall. All these can be visited and are well worth some time.

Oliver Cromwell's House, Ely – This 17th-century house, once the home of Oliver Cromwell, one of England's most famous and powerful leaders, has recently been extensively restored and gives an excellent insight into life in Cromwell's time.

REFRESHMENTS:

The Anchor, Little Downham.
The Plough, Little Downham.
There are numerous possibilities in Ely.

Walks 55 & 56   **CASTOR**   9m (14km)

or 11m (17km)

Maps: OS Sheets Landranger 142; Pathfinder 897 and 918.
Superb Cambridgeshire country, and a fine Nature Reserve.
Start: At 125985, St Kyneburga's Church, Castor

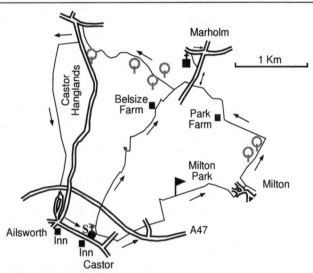

Cross the graveyard, with the church to your right, to reach a street.

The shorter walk turns left to the end of the road. Take the bridleway ahead, crossing the A47 and maintaining direction for a mile to reach a dyke. Turn right, then, after 500 yards, turn left through the wood beside Belsize Farm to reach a track. Turn right, then left beside the dyke. After 500 yards, turn right along a bridleway. Turn left at the road, then left again to reach **St Mary's Church, Marholm** where the longer route is rejoined.

For the longer walk, take the footpath/alley ahead to reach a road. Cross and take the path opposite, following it along the edges of two fields to reach a stile. Do not cross: instead, turn left along the hedge (remaining in the second field) to reach a stile on to the A47. Cross, with great care, and follow the path opposite to a lane. Take the path opposite, going diagonally over a bank and then across a golf course, passing a pond to reach a track. Turn left through a gate and, after 200 yards, turn right along a signed path, following it across Milton Park golf course – the path is waymarked by yellow arrows and large white circles on poles. On the other side of the course, with **Milton Hall** to your left, cross a field to a bridge and turn slightly left to continue to another bridge and a stile. Beyond, follow the waymarked path to the right, going around one field and then between several more. Cross a final field diagonally right and go through a small band of trees to reach a large green area and a cycle path. Follow this, then take the first path on the left, walk through a short alley. Go down Thomas Close, Milton, turning right at the end to reach a post box. Turn left along Carters Close, going through the short alley at the end. Turn left along a track, following it to a gate. Go through and turn right immediately, keeping to the most right-hand path through woodland. Cross a field to the drive of Park Farm. Turn left to the farm, then turn right and follow the Torpel Way for almost a mile to reach a road. Turn right to reach a turning to St Mary's Church, on the left, rejoining the shorter walk.

Take the path beside the churchyard to a road and turn right to the centre of Marholm. Turn right along the road to Castor and, after $1/_2$ mile, turn right along a bridleway (the Torpel Way), following it to a dyke. Bear left with the path, then turn right along the next path on your right (still following the Torpel Way). Follow the path beside several fields and woods, maintaining the same general direction. Finally, bear right beside a wood and yet more fields to reach a road. Turn left to a crossroads. Turn left again and, after 500 yards, turn right along a track signed for the **Castor Hanglands Nature Reserve**. At the end of the track, turn left along a bridleway, following it through the Reserve and maintaining direction to reach the A47. Cross, with care, and follow the path opposite to a road. Turn left into Ailsworth. At the main road, turn left towards Castor, bearing right at the junction. **St Kyneburga's Church** is just under a mile ahead.

POINTS OF INTEREST:

St Mary's Church, Marholm – Originally Norman and still with a Norman tower.
Milton Hall – The Hall, a fine 16th-century building, with later additions, set in pleasant grounds, has belonged to the Fitzwilliam family since the early 1500s.
Castor Hanglands Nature Reserve – The Reserve covers a mixture of grassland, heathland, woodland and scrub and is home to a variety of wildlife.
St Kyneburga's Church, Castor – This 12th-century church – the only one in England dedicated to St Kyneburga – is arguably one of the most important Norman parish churches in Cambridgeshire. The tower is particularly fine.

REFRESHMENTS:
The Fitzwilliam Arms, Marholm.
The Wheatsheaf, Ailsworth.
There are also several possibilities in Castor.

Walk 57   **SAWTRY AND THE GIDDINGS**   9¹/₂m (15km)
Maps: OS Sheets Landranger 142; Pathfinder 939.
A very pleasant long walk through fenland villages and countryside.
Start: At 167836, the parade of shops, Sawtry.

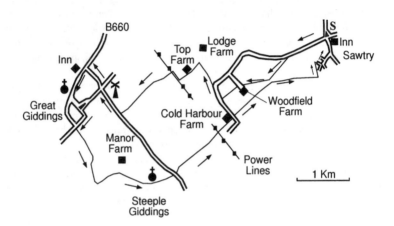

From the shops, take the main road to the Giddings, following it out of Sawtry for about 1,000 yards to reach a track on the left. Take two steps along the track, then cross the bridge on the right and follow a path diagonally across a field to another bridge. Go around the edges of three more fields (and past a bridge), cross another bridge, round two more fields, doing a slight left-hand wiggle between them, and go straight across a field to a road. Turn right to reach a right-hand corner. Take the byway straight ahead, following it to an obvious hole in the hedge on the left, just before coming level with Lodge Farm. Go through the hedge and continue past Top Farm to reach a marker post under the power lines. Turn right and follow the signs around the edge of the field (do not go diagonally across: that is not a footpath). Continue to follow the footpath (not the bridleway) signs, going along the edge of a small wood, then maintaining direction along the edges of two fields, crossing a bridge between them, to reach a lane. Turn right towards the old windmill. At the crossroads, go ahead to reach the main road (B660) and turn left, with care, into **Great Gidding**.

Turn left at the crossroads in the centre of the village and follow a lane around to the right to reach a road. Walk up the road for about 100 yards, then take the unsigned track to the left, just before a long narrow field. Continue along field edges to reach a stile on the left. Do not cross: instead, turn right, away from the stile and walk to a bridge. Cross and follow the obvious paths through the next three fields, then cross back over the brook. In the next field, turn slightly left, then take the path to the right across the field. Go diagonally across the next field, heading for the corner of the trees to the left of the steeple top. Walk beside the trees, then along a track to reach a lane in **Steeple Gidding**. Follow the lane to a road and take the footpath opposite, following it through fields for about $1^1/_4$ miles to Cold Harbour Farm. Cross a lane and follow the signed path across a field, heading for the left-hand edge of a clump of trees. Cross the next field to reach a drain (and a bridge). Do not cross the bridge but turn right, following the edges of two fields, then the opposite edge of the next to reach a track. Cross the track and take the path ahead to reach a bridge just before the houses on your left. Cross and follow the field edge to the side of a large white house. Turn right and walk through a housing estate to the main road. Turn left, passing the **church** on the way back to the start.

POINTS OF INTEREST:

Great Gidding – St Michael's Church has a spire and some very large and colourful stained-glass windows. It is basically from the late 13th century, though the south doorway is thought to be early 13th-century and the style of the tower dates it from between 1290 and 1350. Much of the wooden interior decoration is 17th-century. The church is the site of various concerts and theatrical performances throughout the year.
Steeple Gidding – St Andrew's Church was built in the same period and of the same style as that at Great Gidding, but is now redundant and slightly unkempt.
All Saints' Church, Sawtry – Built in 1880 by Sir A. Blomfield, the church has no tower or steeple but a very steep and detailed bellcote. It houses a number of interesting artefacts including outstandingly good brasses and pieces from Sawtry Abbey.

REFRESHMENTS:
The Fox and Hounds, Great Gidding.
There is plenty of choice in Sawtry.

Walk 58   RAMPTON   10m (16km)

Maps: OS Sheets Landranger 154; Pathfinder 961 and 982.
A very pleasant mixture of fenland and water courses.
Start: At 426680, the Village Green, High Street, Rampton.

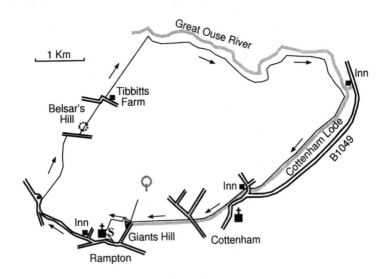

From the Green, walk along the road towards Willingham for $^1/_2$ mile. Then, just past the buildings on the corner, take the public byway to your right, following it to a road. Turn right for about 50 yards, then turn left along a path, following it over **Belsar's Hill** to a road near Tibbitts Farm and maintaining direction along a track to reach the **Great Ouse River**.

Turn right and walk beside the river for about 3 miles, then, just before the main road (the B1049) at Upper Cuts (follow the path to the road and turn right for the inn), turn right along **Cottenham Lode**.

Walk along the right-hand embankment of Cottenham Lode for about 3 miles, passing an inn and crossing two lanes along the way. At a corner of the Lode, just before the end, drop down off the embankment and follow the arrowed path across a small bridge. Continue along the path, going around a wood and an orchard and into **Rampton Park**. Walk across the Park (to visit **All Saints' Church** take the small path on your right and to visit **Giant's Hill** walk across the field to reach an information board in its far corner). On the other side of Rampton Park you will reach a road: turn right to return to the centre of Rampton.

POINTS OF INTEREST:

Belsar's Hill – A prehistoric earthwork consisting of a single oval-shaped bank and ditch measuring 800 ft long and 750 ft wide.

Great Ouse River – The Great Ouse River Valley provides some of the most interesting and attractive countryside in the county. In such an expanse of dry arable land as Cambridgeshire, the river and the water-filled gravel pits provide a rare and valuable habitat for water species. The river's flood meadows provide a permanent grassland habitat rich in mature trees and wild flower species such as cowslips, crosswort and salad burnet.

Cottenham Lode – Although a man-made feature this wide channel of water has become a natural habitat for a wide diversity of water species including many reeds, rushes and marsh plants, a number a species of insects, most notably dragonflies and butterflies. It also attracts a variety of birds including coots, moorhens and swans.

Rampton Park – The Park and the surrounding grassland is exceedingly rich in wildlife due to the variety of habitats – mature oaks, grassland, bramble, water and marsh areas. As well as the 47 plant species found here, bird species include warblers, spotted flycatchers, kestrels and owls, and mammals include voles, shrew, mice, hedgehogs, foxes and pipistrelle bats.

All Saints' Church, Rampton – The church has an unusual appearance as it is thatched. It dates primarily from the Norman period and does have some noteworthy features, particularly inside.

Giant's Hill, Rampton – Giant's Hill or Rampton Castle is a superb example of an ancient earthworks. The castle was built in the 12th century by King Stephen to try and control the rampaging Essex Baron, Geoffrey de Mandeville. The castle is complete with moat, ramparts and all aspects of a mini village – cottages, fields, etc.

REFRESHMENTS:
The Black Horse, Rampton.
The Twenty Pence Inn, Upper Cuts.

Walk 59   WATERBEACH AND UPWARE   10m (16km)

Maps: OS Sheets Landranger 154; Pathfinder 982 and 961.

A riverside walk along the River Cam, part of the famous Cambridge to Ely Path.

Start: At 507657, Bottisham Lock, Waterbeach.

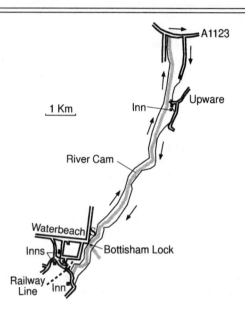

From Bottisham Lock, just outside Waterbeach, walk to the **River Cam**, turn left and follow the riverside path roughly northwards. Follow the path for about 4 miles to reach the A1123. There, leave the footpath, using the road bridge, with care, to cross the river. Continue along the road for about 500 yards to reach a track crossing the road. Turn right down this track, following it past a small wood. At the far end of the wood, follow the path around to the right, and then walk around the edge of a field to reach a stile on the far side. Cross this and the field beyond, following the right-hand hedge, to reach a road.

Turn right, passing an inn and following the sign to reach the riverside path. Follow this path to a road. Turn right along the road for about 500 yards, then turn right along a signed track to return to the river. Turn left and follow the river south towards Cambridge. After about 3 miles you will reach Bottisham Lock again. Stay on the eastern bank of the river and maintain direction for a mile to reach a road. Turn right and cross a road bridge over the River Cam. Continue along the road for a mile into the centre of Waterbeach, passing the **Church of St John** and the Baptist Church on your left. Retrace your steps along the road and take the path on the left, just out of the town, signed for Bottisham Lock, Dimmock Cote and Ely. Follow the path, and then the riverbank, back to the lock. An alternative route from Waterbeach takes the road opposite the Baptist Church: follow this to its end and turn right along Bannold Road, following the road back to the lock.

POINTS OF INTEREST:

River Cam – The Cam, a tributary of the Great Ouse River, is one of the most beautiful and atmospheric of rivers in England. Meandering through the dry, flat farmland of the fens, the river provides a striking contrast both in scenery and in its wildlife, this ranging from reeds to water-lilies, pondskaters to kingfishers. Due to its popularity, the river also has many delightful riverside inns and teashops, and a number of excellent boating opportunities.

St John's Church, Waterbeach – The church was originally built around 1200, but has since been altered and added to in the 17th, 18th and 19th centuries. As a consequence it is now rather a mix of styles.

REFRESHMENTS:

The Five Miles From Anywhere, No Hurry Inn, Upware.
The Riverside Inn, Clayhithe.
The Sun Inn, Waterbeach.
The White Horse, Waterbeach.

Maps: OS Sheets Landranger 142; Pathfinder 939 and 918.
Long walks to some pretty villages and churches.
Start: At 163894, the High Street, Stilton.

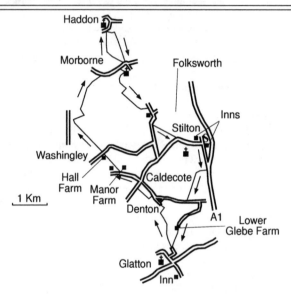

Walk down the High Street towards the A1 to reach a stile on the right just before the
main road. Cross and follow a track to its end, then turn right and follow a field edge
beside a golf course. At the end of the course, cross a dyke, turn left and follow field
edges to a road. Turn left for 500 yards to the track of Lower Glebe Farm, on the right.
Follow it past the derelict farm, maintaining direction along a field edge. At the end,
follow the permissive path on the right up the field to a byway. Turn left and continue
along a lane to visit **St Nicholas' Church, Glatton**. Retrace your steps and follow the
byway to a road. Turn right and follow the road left, and then right, to reach a path on
the left. Follow the path to a road. Turn right towards Caldecote, then first left and
follow a road for about 500 yards to reach a path on the right, just after Manor Farm.
Go down a field, turn left at the bottom and walk beside, and then into, a wood.
Follow the path past Shingley Lake, then take the left-hand fork and cross a stile into

Hall Farm. Follow the drive to a road and cross to the path on the left. Follow the path to a stile. Cross and turn left towards a house and road. Just before reaching the house, turn right along a signed path. After about 200 yards, turn left through an opening in the hedge, and follow a bridleway around the top of a field. Maintain direction to a road and turn right, passing **All Saints' Church**, into Morborne.

The short walk retraces steps along the road and takes the first footpath on the left. Follow the waymarkers across and around fields to a wider path at the top of the ridge. Bear right along this path, then, almost immediately, take the path on your left, following it into Folksworth, arriving beside **St Helen's Church**. Walk through the graveyard and turn right along the road into the village. Follow the main road around to the right, then left, then take the first road on the left. At its end, turn right (Blackmans Road) and walk through a housing estate to Townsend Way and a path almost straight ahead. Follow the path across two fields to a road at Stilton. Turn left and follow the road past **St Mary's Church** and back into the village centre.

The long walk also retraces steps, but takes the second signed path on the right. Follow this path beside and across fields into Haddon, arriving by **St Mary's Church**. Now, from the same corner of the field beside the church, take the other path (opposite the church) to the gate in the far corner. Go through the other gate and follow a path beside the fields back into Morbourne. Now follow the short walk back to Stilton.

POINTS OF INTEREST:

St Mary's Church, Stilton – This tall church dates from the early 13th century, though the present chancel was begun in 1808 and not completed until 1859.

Stilton – High Street has a number of interesting 17th-century buildings, the most obvious being the Bell Inn, which still retains its original ironwork decorations.

St Nicholas' Church, Glatton – Built in the 13th century, this solid church has a beautiful array of battlements, friezes, pinnacles and stone animals.

All Saints' Church, Morborne – Originally built between 1140 and 1280 this small country church has a rather unusual 17th-century brick tower.

St Mary's Church, Haddon – The church is mainly early 13th-century and has a very impressive Norman chancel arch.

St Helen's Church, Folksworth – A small, inconspicuous medieval church with a bellcote.

REFRESHMENTS:
The Addison Arms, Glatton.
The Fox, Folksworth.
There is also plenty of choice in Stilton.

Walk 62   **HORSEHEATH**   10m (16km)

Maps: OS Sheets Landranger 154; Pathfinder 1004, 1005, 1027 and 1028.

A long, but interesting, walk through fine countryside.

Start: At 613472, the three-way road junction in Horseheath.

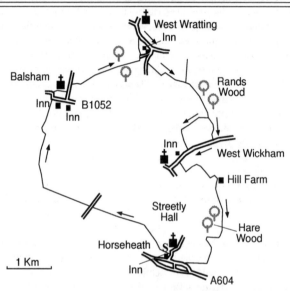

Take the road to West Wickham and, almost immediately, take the footpath on the left signed for Streetly Hall. Follow the path through and around fields to reach a wide bridleway. Turn left and follow the bridleway for about 2 miles, crossing a road at a dip in the landscape. When the **Icknield Way** is signed to the right, turn along it, following it for about 2 miles into Balsham. (Turn right along the main street to reach the inn.) The walk takes the lane straight ahead, following it around a right-hand corner to **Holy Trinity Church**. Go through the churchyard (along the right-hand path) to reach a road. Turn left for about 200 yards to reach a footpath for West Wratting on the right. Take the right-hand path, following it across a field. Cross a stile and walk to the right around the next field. Continue as waymarked, going across two fields, through woodland and across a field to a lane. Turn right, but soon turn left along a footpath, following it to West Wratting High Street. **St Andrew's Church** is

120

about 500 yards to the left. The walk turns right. Take the next road on the right and at the end of the buildings, take the path signed for West Wickham on the left.

Follow the path along the edge of **West Wratting Park** to reach a sharp corner and an obvious path going diagonally to the right. Follow this path beside Rands Wood. At the end of the wood, follow the waymarked path (then the track) into West Wickham. Whether you continue along the track or turn right, then left on any of the paths does not matter. At the road, turn right into the centre of West Wickham to reach **St Mary's Church**, passing the inn. Retrace your steps along the road to the first signed footpath on the right. Take this, following it around a right-angled bend to the left, and then around one to the right, to reach a concrete track. Turn left along the track to Hill Farm. Walk around the buildings and take the obvious path heading southwards, following it beside fields and past Hare Wood. Turn right along the bottom of the wood and take the next obvious path on the left, following it to a track and then on to the telegraph poles. Here, turn right and follow the path under the wires to reach a road. Turn right for about 300 yards to reach the start. The inn is ahead: for **All Saints' Church**, turn right.

POINTS OF INTEREST:

Icknield Way – A famous prehistoric highway linking Salisbury Plain to the Wash.
Holy Trinity Church, Balsham – A confusing mix of styles and periods. The tower seems mid-13th century, the chancel mid-14th century, and the aisle windows mid-15th century.
St Andrew's Church, West Wratting – Originally built in the 14th century in English Gothic style, but suffered many 'disfiguring' changes in the 18th century and was subsequently much restored and rebuilt in the 19th century.
West Wratting Park – This fine red-brick mansion was built in 1730.
St Mary's Church, West Wickham – A small, sheltered church of flint and pebble rubble is almost entirely of Perpendicular English Gothic with a Decorated chancel.
All Saints' Church, Horseheath – Mainly Decorated English Gothic architecture, but with a nave in Perpendicular style, the height, and the light from the tall windows, of which make the interior a very pleasant place.

REFRESHMENTS:

The Old Red Lion, Horseheath.
The Black Bull, Balsham.
The Bells, Balsham.
The Chestnut Tree Inn, West Wratting.
The White Horse Inn, West Wickham.

Walk 63　　SAWSTON AND THE SHELFORDS　　10m (16km)

Maps: OS Sheets Landranger 154; Pathfinder 1004 and 1027.

A pleasant walk mainly through large villages.

Start: At 485495, in the High Street, Sawston.

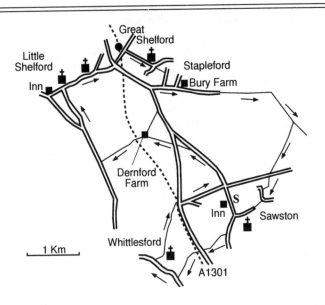

Walk southwards, passing St Mary the Virgin's Church and Sawston Hall and continuing for about a mile to reach a footpath for Whittlesford on the right, opposite Prince William Way. Follow this path, crossing the A1301 and the railway, with care. Cross the River Cam and continue to the end of the path. Turn left through a farm and follow the road to a T-junction. Turn right along the main road and then right into Church Lane. Now take the footpath on the left, going along an alley. Bear right, then turn right to reach **St Mary's and St Andrew's Church**. Retrace your steps along the path, but soon take the tarmac footpath on the right, following it over the Cam to reach the railway. Cross the railway and main road, again with care, and take the road to Sawston. Beyond the school, turn left along the road to Great Shelford, following it for almost a mile, then turn left along a footpath, following it across a field to reach the main road again. Cross, with care, and take the path ahead around a field. Go

122

diagonally across the next two fields to reach Dernford Farm. Go through the buildings to a lane and bear left along it, crossing the railway again. Follow the signed path ahead keeping beside, but not inside, a field to reach a road. Turn right and, where the road forks, take the left-hand branch, turning right in the village to reach the inn and **All Saints' Church**.

Continue along the road towards Great Shelford, passing **St Mary the Virgin's Church** and continuing into the village. At the fork, take the right-hand branch to reach the A1301. Cross this and the railway beyond, with care, to reach Mingle Lane, on the right. Follow the lane for just under a mile to reach **St Andrew's Church**, Stapleford. Continue along the road and, just round the corner, turn left along an alley (Vicarage Lane). At its end, turn right along a road, following it to a T-junction. Turn left and follow the road to a corner. Take the footpath ahead, through Bury Farm, following it to reach a distinct change of direction, at the end of a track marked by a bridge and two stiles. Bear right along the track for about $1/_2$ mile, then take the footpath on the right, following it to a road. Turn right, but soon go along Lynton Way, on the left. Half-way down the road, take the path on the right, crossing a park and going through a play area to reach a small parking area. Leave along the road, then turn left and walk to the end of The Green Road. At the end, turn right to reach a signpost, then take the road into Sawston. Do not follow the tarmac path round by the houses. Continue along the road, passing the church. It is now just a short step, to the right, back to the start.

POINTS OF INTEREST:

Church of St Mary and St Andrew, Whittlesford – Almost entirely Norman, with some work from the 14th and 18th centuries.

All Saints' Church, Little Shelford – A small church in an interesting mixture of styles. Inside there are some excellent sculptures and monuments.

St Mary the Virgin's Church, Great Shelford – Mainly early 15th-century, though the tower was rebuilt in the late 1700s after the earlier one had collapsed.

St Andrew's Church, Stapleford – A small flint church with noteworthy painted nave and chancel ceilings.

REFRESHMENTS:

Tickell Arms, Whittlesford.
The Sycamore House, Little Shelford.
The Tree, Stapleford.
The Longbow, Stapleford.
The Rose, Stapleford.
There are also numerous possibilities in Sawston.

Maps: OS Sheets Landranger 154; Pathfinder 1026 and 1003.
A long walk including a lovely Nature Reserve and wildlife.
Start: At 378468, Holy Trinity Church, Meldreth.

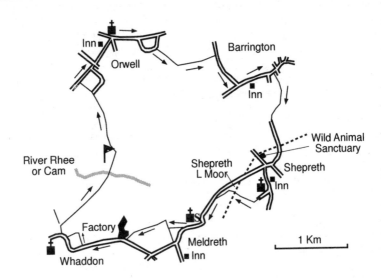

From the church walk about 200 yards along the road towards the town, then take the footpath on the right, following it to a track. Turn right and, at the end of the track, turn left and follow a path beside one field and across two more to reach a track. Turn left to a road. Turn right then after about $1/2$ mile, take the signed path on the right, following it away from the road and around several field edges. Go through a clump of trees and turn left to reach a road. St Mary's Church, Waddon is 300 yards along the road. The walk continues by turning right along a track. After about 200 yards, turn right along a signed footpath, follow it around field edges to the River Rhee/Cam. Cross the river and follow the track ahead through a golf course, joining another track, but maintaining direction. Where the track becomes a path, walk ahead along the edge of a field. Now maintain direction, keeping the church on your right until the path ends at a track. Turn right, then walk about a mile up Town Green Road into Orwell to reach **St Andrew's Church** and the High Street. Turn right along the High

.treet, following it for almost a mile. Now take the small road on the right to Malton and Meldreth. Now take the signed footpath on the left, following a track, and then a ath, along field edges for almost a mile to reach a road. Turn right and walk into Barrington, following the road beside the lovely large green to **All Saints' Church**. Retrace your steps to the footpath for Shepreth, on the left, beside the village store. Follow the path to cross the river, then cross a field beside trees and go diagonally cross another field, under the telegraph poles, to reach a lane. Turn left, crossing the ailway, with care, into Angle Lane, passing the **Wild Animal Sanctuary** on the ight. At the main village road, turn right and then take the next left (Meldreth Road). Follow the road around to the left to reach All Saints' Church. Go through the hurchyard to reach a lane, on the far side, and turn right. Follow the lane to the orner, then turn right along a signed footpath, following it to a stile. Cross and go diagonally across a field and under a railway bridge. Continue through the **Shepreth L Moor Nature Reserve**, following the well-trodden path. On reaching a road, bear eft to walk parallel with it until you can go no further. Now go on to the road and turn eft, following the road for about a mile to return to Holy Trinity Church, Meldreth.

POINTS OF INTEREST:

St Andrew's Church, Orwell – The clunch for this pebble and clunch rubble 12th – 4th-century church was quarried in the village.

All Saints' Church, Barrington – This large church dates mainly from the 13th and 4th centuries, though it seems to have been altered many times.

Wild Animal Sanctuary, Shepreth – Housing animals from turtles and tortoises to monkeys and minks, pigs and cows, the Sanctuary, which has areas to pet and feed the animals, is open all year.

Shepreth L Moor Nature Reserve – An L-shaped area of marshy meadowland that has now almost disappeared from southern Cambridgeshire. The drier areas are characteristic chalk grasslands, home to bee and common spotted orchids, cowslips, harebells and green woodpeckers. The wetland areas are created by the underlying Goult Clay, and are a rare home to flowers such as the marsh orchid and the very rare slender-flowered spike rush and parsley-leaved dropwort. Trout, roach, pike and stickleback live in the clean streams.

REFRESHMENTS:
The British Queen, Meldreth.
The Chequers, Orwell.
The Royal Oak, Barrington.
The Plough, Shepreth.

Walk 65   **BARRINGTON**   10m (16km)

Maps: OS Sheets Landranger 154; Pathfinder 1026, 1027, 1004 and 1003.

Lovely countryside, villages, churches and views.

Start: At 397499, All Saints' Church, Barrington.

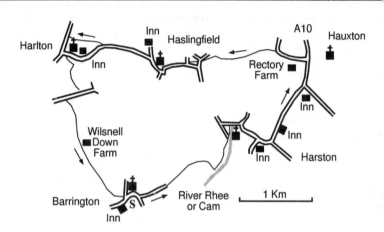

From **All Saints' Church, Barrington** take the road to Foxton, on the left, following the road until it turns right. Here, continue ahead along Glebe Way. At the end, follow the track ahead and, at the buildings, take the signed path slightly to the right. Follow the path to the river. Turn left and follow the path to a road. Turn right into Harston, passing **All Saints' Church, Harston** on your right. On reaching the A10, keep ahead with care, following the road for about a mile into Hauxton. There, turn left along a small lane almost opposite a road. (**St Edmund's Church, Hauxton** is 300 yards along this road.) Follow the lane, going straight ahead along a bridleway when the lane turns sharp right. Follow the bridleway for just over a mile, then cross the River Cam/Rhee to reach a track on the outskirts of Haslingfield. Turn left and walk across the recreation grounds towards the pavilion. At the main road, turn right. After a mile having rounded **All Saints' Church, Haslingfield**, take the road on the left for Harlton.

Follow the road for just under a mile, with excellent views of the University's radio telescopes, then, just before reaching the houses, turn right along a footpath following it along the backs of houses, then across one field and along the edges of two more fields (the right-hand edge in the first and the left-hand edge in the second) to reach a road. Turn left and walk around the duckpond. Now take the left-hand road to reach the **Church of the Assumption of the Blessed Virgin Mary, Harlton** and the village. Take the track directly opposite the church (signed for Barrington), following it through a farmyard. On the far side of the buildings, turn left and take the path running along the backs of the houses. At the next stile turn right (as indicated) along a grassy track. Head uphill towards the trees, turning slightly left mid-way up the slope. At the top of the hill, go through a wood, then turn right along the top edge of a field. Turn left and walk downhill. Just before the buildings, the path bends around to the right, then to the left: continue along it, after the buildings going straight ahead beside two fields to reach a lane. Turn left and walk back into Barrington: the Church will be to your left, the village green to your right.

POINTS OF INTEREST:

All Saints' Church, Barrington – This large church dates mainly from the 13th and 14th centuries, though it seems to have been altered many times since. The upper half of the tower is of a later date than the lower part, the nave was widened in both the 14th and 15th centuries, the north porch and north chapel are 15th-century additions and some of the aisle windows are as late as the 19th century.

All Saints Church, Harston – Mainly of the Perpendicular and Decorated styles of English Gothic architecture, except for the chancel which was rebuilt in 1853.

St Edmund's Church, Hauxton – Built of clunch rubble, this church has some Norman features, most notably the nave, the chancel and the chancel arch.

All Saints Church, Haslingfield – Mainly of the Perpendicular and Decorated styles of English Gothic architecture, but retaining a very typical Norman frieze along the outer walls of the chancel, a 13th-century chancel arch and an 18th-century lead roof to the porch. The interior is also interesting: there are some lovely stained glass windows, a pretty painted chancel roof and several monuments.

Church of the Assumption of the Blessed Virgin Mary, Harlton – The beauty of this church lies in the interior, where its tall and upright proportions can be seen.

REFRESHMENTS:

The Royal Oak, Barrington.
The English Gentleman, Hauxton.
The Little Rose, Haslingfield.
Hare and Hounds, Harlton.
There are also several possibilities in Harston.

Walk 66   THE PAPWORTHS   10m (16km)

Maps: OS Sheets Landranger 153; Pathfinder 981.

A fine walk – interest all the way.

Start: At 285630, the Post Office, Papworth Everard.

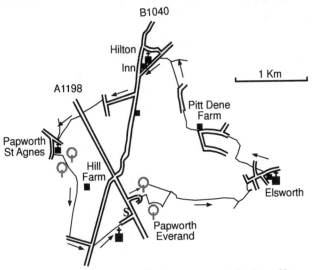

Walk along the main road, towards Huntingdon, then turn right along Chequers Lane, immediately after the factory shop, and before the Green. Follow the lane to the corner, then go ahead along the footpath through woodland. Beyond the wood, walk beside a field and then, at its end, turn right to walk past an orchard. At the woodland, turn left to walk beside the wood, continuing across fields to the edge of the small wood ahead. Turn right along a track, following it for over a mile to meet another track just before Avenue Farm. Here turn left and walk around to the right to reach a road. Turn right into the centre of Elsworth. To visit **Holy Trinity Church**, take the next road on the right, then the first turning on the left. To continue the walk, take the path across the Green, from opposite the inn, and, on the far side, cross the street and take the signed footpath ahead, following it along a field edge and around the next field to reach a track. Turn right to the end of the field. Cross a dyke to a track and turn left. Where the track turns left, keep left to Pitt Dene Farm. Walk through the farm, then maintain direction along a concrete track, passing the barn. Now, just around the corner, take the grassy track on the right, following it down a field and along the edges of two more fields to reach a track. Turn left to reach a road in Hilton. Cross the road to visit the **Hilton Turf Maze**. Now walk southwards along the road to reach **St Mary Magdalene's Church** and the B1040. Turn left for about 500 yards, then cross, with care, and turn right along a track. Follow this for $^1/_2$ mile, then, at the end, turn slightly right to maintain direction along a path beside the field edge, following it to the main road (the A1198). Cross, with care, bearing slightly left to reach a footpath. Follow this grassy track to reach a lane in front of **St John's Church, Papworth St Agnes**. Turn right and, at the end of the lane, turn left along a road, walking to the second signed footpath on the left, opposite a path on the right. Follow the path across a field, turning at the yellow post in the middle to reach the top right-hand corner. (You may wish to find the far stile, so as to know where you are heading, before entering the field and meeting the resident bull.) Follow the path beyond the stile through a wood and towards a farm. Now bear right along the path which starts just before the farm, following it past the trees and down to the road (using a concrete track and, finally, a grassy path). Turn left to reach the B1040. Cross, with care, and take the signed path for Papworth Everard slightly to the left. Cross a field, then go around the woods to a bridge. Cross, turn right and head uphill to a stile and **St Peter's Church**. Follow the road ahead to the main road and turn left to return to the start.

POINTS OF INTEREST:

Holy Trinity Church, Elsworth – Dating from the 1300s, this church displays the finery of the Decorated style, especially the battlements and pinnacles.

Hilton Turf Maze, Hilton – This is one of only eight surviving turf mazes in England. Cut in 1660 by William Sparrow, the maze is of a popular medieval design, possibly originating at Chartres Cathedral in France.

St Mary Magdalene's Church, Hilton – Apart from the west tower which is 14th-century, the church is built entirely in the Perpendicular style of English Gothic architecture of which it is a very good example.

St John's Church, Papworth St Agnes – The church's origins are unknown. Some parts appear to be 14th-century, but the tower, nave and chancel are 19th-century.

St Peter's Church, Papworth Everard – After the destruction of the old tower in 1741 by a hurricane, the church now dates almost completely from 1850.

REFRESHMENTS:
The Poacher, Elsworth.
Prince of Wales, Hilton.
Kisby's Hut, Papworth Everard.

BOURN

Maps: OS Sheets Landranger 153; Pathfinder 1003.
A lovely 'Windmill Walk'.
Start: At 325564, the Golden Lion Inn, Bourn.

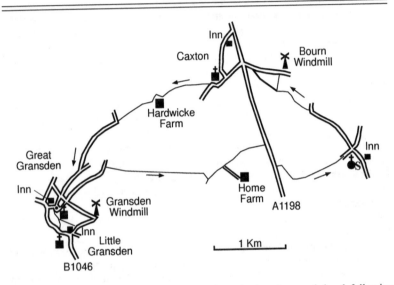

Walk northwards along the road to the corner, then take the minor road ahead, following it for almost a mile to reach a sharp right-hand bend. Here, take the signed footpath on the left crossing a lawn and a bridge and going through a garden to reach a field. (If it very wet please avoid this walk as it ruins the lawn.) Follow the path around the field edges, walking beside a dyke. On reaching a bridge, on the left, take the path across the field on the right to visit **Bourn Windmill**. Return to the stream and continue beside it to reach a road in Caxton. Turn left to reach the main road (the A1198). Cross, with care, and take the road ahead (and slightly right), following it for about 500 yards to reach **St Andrew's Church**. Walk through the churchyard to rejoin the road and turn right to the corner. Here, take the bridleway ahead, following this grassy track beside fields to Hardwicke Farm. Follow the signed path through the garden and around the house to the drive. Turn right along the signed bridleway, following it to a road in Great Gransden, the track becoming a lane as you near the village. At the road, turn right to the roundabout at the village centre. Turn left to **St Bartholomew's**

Church. Follow the path through the graveyard to reach a stream at the bottom of a slight hill. Cross the stream and follow the tarmac path ahead to reach the B1046 in Little Gransden. Turn left and take the next right to visit **St Peter and St Paul's Church**. Return to the main road, turn right, and take the next road on the left (Primrose Hill), following it to **Gransden Windmill**. Turn left for about 500 yards to the outskirts of Great Gransden, then turn right along Sandy Road, following it for just under a mile. Now turn right along a footpath immediately before the buildings. Walk beside a field and through another field. Go over a bridge, across a field and beside another field, then bear slightly left along a track. Walk beside several fields to reach another track. Turn right, then, after walking around a barn, take the signed path on the left. At the barrier in the road, turn left through a clump of trees, then follow the path across two fields. Turn right along a track, continuing ahead where the track bends to reach a road. Turn right and walk to the other side of the woods on the left, then follow a path around the corner of a field to reach a path junction. Go ahead, following the bridleway to its end, then following Riddly Lane into Bourn. Turn right up Church Street to visit the **Church of St Helena and St Mary**, then go back down Church Street and turn first right to return to the inn.

POINTS OF INTEREST:

Bourn Windmill – This post mill dates to pre-Civil War times and is open one Sunday each month from April to September.

St Andrew's Church, Caxton – St Andrew's Church is mainly late 14th-century, but much restored. The tower and chancel are original.

St Bartholomew's Church, Great Gransden – Built of brown cobbles, this Perpendicular church has a tower topped with a spike and a roof adorned with figures.

St Peter and St Paul's Church, Little Gransden – The church was almost entirely restored in the 19th century, yet still looks as though it were built around 1400.

Gransden Windmill – This post mill is a scheduled ancient monument. Built from 1614 onwards, the mill last worked in 1911, but was beautifully restored in 1982-3.

St Helena and St Mary's Church, Bourn – Built of pebble rubble between the 13th and 14th centuries. The tower was built in the mid-13th century and is complete with buttresses, bell-openings, battlements and a fine crooked lead spire.

REFRESHMENTS:

The Golden Lion, Bourn.
The Cross Keys Inn, Caxton.
The Crown and Cushion, Great Gransden.
The Chequers Inn, Little Gransden.

Walk 68   **WITCHFORD**   10m (16km)

Maps: OS Sheets Landranger 143; Pathfinder 941 and 961.

A walk through typical fenland.

Start: At 504787, St Andrew's Church, Witchford.

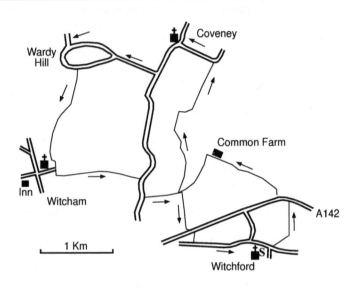

From **St Andrew's Church, Witchford**, walk eastwards along the road for 100 yards to reach a signed byway on the left. Follow this to the A142. Turn left beside the road for 200 yards, then cross, with care, to reach a byway. (Take care not to take the footpath by mistake: the path is about half-way to the byway.) Follow the byway (a track) around to the left, continuing along it when it turns into a sandy track. Go past Common Farm, then take the next signed byway on the left (the second one you have past). Follow the byway along the edge of a small dyke to reach another byway (a grassy track) on the right. Follow this byway north towards Coveney. On meeting another track, turn right and then turn left with the track to reach a road. Turn left and follow the road to reach a junction in Coveney. The **Church of St Peter-ad-Vincula** is to the right.

To continue the walk, turn left and take the next road on the right. Follow the road through Wardy Hill. On the other side of the village, as the road veers right, keep straight ahead along a track, following it around to the left, through the farm buildings, to reach a wide grassy track on the right. Follow this public byway into Witcham. At the end, turn left, then right into Headley Lane. About 100 yards along the lane turn right to reach **St Martin's Church** and Witcham village centre.

To continue the walk, return to Headley Lane and turn right along it. At the end of the lane, turn left along a public byway, following it for just over a mile to reach a road. Turn right, then take the next public byway on the left. Follow this byway beside a dyke to reach a grassy track on the right. Take this track, following it to the A142. Cross, with care, and walk down the shaded track ahead to reach a road. Turn left and follow the road into Witchford.

POINTS OF INTEREST:

St Andrew's Church, Witchford – Built across the 13th and 14th centuries, this church is mainly in the Decorated style of English Gothic architecture, but is surprisingly low, with a low-roofed chancel and a short tower.

The Church of St Peter-ad-Vincula, Coveney – This small church was built mainly in the 13th century, but the tower was added at a later date, as was the porch and the north doorway. The chancel also appears to have been lengthened at a later date.

St Martin's Church, Witcham – This small church dates from the 13th and 14th centuries, but has been much repaired and added to at later dates.

REFRESHMENTS:

The Shoulder of Mutton, Witchford.
The White Horse Inn, Witcham.

Walk 69   CATWORTH   10m (16km)

Maps: OS Sheets Landranger 153; Pathfinder 959 and 980.

Fine villages and interesting churches.

Start: At 085732, the Racehorse Inn, Catworth.

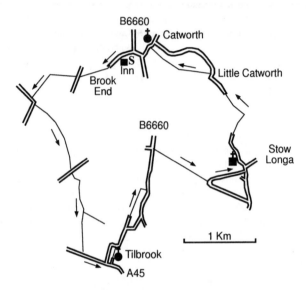

Take the lane running in front of the inn, following it downhill and to its end at Brook End. Take the signed bridleway on the right, following it to a crossing track. Go straight on to reach the end of the bridleway. Turn left and walk along another bridleway for about $^1/_2$ mile to reach the corner of a road. Turn left along yet another signed bridleway, following it beside several fields and passing under an old railway line to reach a road. Cross and continue along the bridleway opposite, following it across a field and up the side of the next field. At the top of the field, turn right along a tree-lined bridleway. Follow this lovely grassy track for just over a mile to reach a road, taking care towards the end to keep ahead and over a bridge, and not to turn left. At the road (the A45), turn left and walk, with care, into Tilbrook.

In the village, go past the road to Catworth, then take the second road on the left to reach **All Saints' Church**. Follow the path straight through the churchyard to reach a road. Turn right, following the road over a bridge and continuing along it until it bends to the right and a 'dead end' is signed ahead. Take this lane and, at its end, continue ahead along a path (slightly overgrown). After $^1/_2$ mile you will reach a track: cross this and continue to reach a road (the B660). Turn left and follow the road, with care, for about $^1/_2$ mile, passing Tanglewood House to reach a bridleway on the right, opposite the road to Covington. Follow the bridleway along field edges to reach a track. Continue ahead, along the track, following it around to the left. Now keep straight ahead to reach a road in Stow Longa. Turn left, then take the next left, following Church Walk to **St Botolph's Church**.

Retrace your steps along Church Walk and turn left. Follow the lane, and then a bridleway going ahead, and then around to the left to reach a junction. Turn left, but very soon turn right and walk to a lane. Go down the lane until it bends at some houses. Here, go between the houses and follow the path ahead. Continue along the path into Catworth, arriving beside **St Leonard's Church**. Turn left along the road, then right along the next road to return to the inn.

POINTS OF INTEREST:

All Saints' Church, Tilbrook – Mainly built in the late 13th century, this church is a very good example of the Decorated style of English Gothic architecture, though other styles can also be seen.

St Botolph's Church, Stow Longa – This large church, situated just outside the village and commanding a fine view of the surrounding countryside, is in a mixture of Early English, Decorated and Perpendicular styles.

St Leonard's Church, Catsworth – Apart from the piscina in the chancel and the south doorway, which are Early English, this church dates from the late 14th century and is Perpendicular in architectural style.

REFRESHMENTS:
The Racehorse Inn, Catworth.
The White Horse Inn, Tilbrook.

Walk 70   SAWSTON   11m (18km)

Maps: OS Sheets Landranger 154; Pathfinder 1004 and 1027.

A fine long walk with a variety of interest.

Start: At 488492, St Mary the Virgin's Church, Sawston.

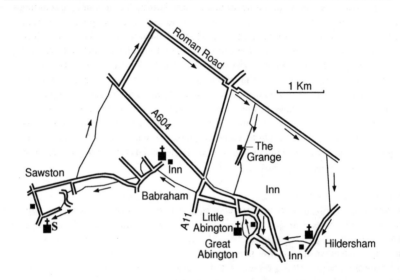

From **St Mary the Virgin's Church**, in the centre of Sawston, walk eastwards to the end of the road. Turn left to the end of The Green Road. Turn left to reach a playing field, on the right. Cross the field to Lynton Way, and turn left to reach the Sawston/Babraham Road. Turn right and follow the road to the end of the buildings on the left. Here, take the signed footpath on the left, following it to a track. Turn left for about 20 yards, then take the path ahead, following it to the main road (the A604). Turn right for almost 200 yards, then cross, with care, and follow the track on the left uphill for about a mile to reach a Roman Road. Turn right along the road, crossing the A11 after about 1¹/₂ miles.

Continue along the Roman Road to reach the next track on the right (after a further 1¹/₄ miles). Follow this track to a road and turn right. Follow the road into Hildersham, then, after passing Holy Trinity Church, on your right, take the footpath on the right, just before the river. (Continue straight ahead for the inn.) Follow the

ell-trodden path to the A604. Cross, with care, walk beside the house and turn right
ong the road to reach a T-junction in Great Abington. Turn left along the road to
ach a path on the right to St Mary's Church, Great Abington. Take the path beside
e churchyard, following it to reach a road in Little Abington. Turn left to reach
Mary's Church, Little Abington.

Continue along the road, going around a sharp left-hand corner and continuing
estwards to reach the A11. Cross, with care, and follow the track opposite to reach
e main village road in Babraham. Turn right to reach the inn. The walk turns slightly
ft, taking the small alley almost ahead. Walk past **Babraham Pocket Park** and
wn a lane, passing **Babraham Hall** to reach **St Peter's Church**. Retrace your steps
ong the lane, soon reaching a stile on the right. Cross and follow a path along the
eld edge, going diagonally across the next field and through the school grounds to
ach a road. Turn right and then take the next right. At the corner, take the signed
otpath to Sawston. Follow this obvious path, crossing a road, and continuing (as
dicated) towards Sawston. On reaching the housing estate, follow the path for as
ng as possible to reach a signpost at the end of The Green Road. Now retrace your
eps, soon returning to the start.

OINTS OF INTEREST:

Mary the Virgin's Church, Sawston – Built of pebble and stone rubble, but with
atures from a wide variety of eras. Close by is Sawston Hall, a fine Elizabethan
ansion set in superb grounds. It is the only one-courtyard house in the county and
e only one built of clunch as opposed to brick.

abraham Pocket Park – Very small, a true 'pocket' park.

abraham Hall – Built around 1830 in Jacobean style.

Peter's Church, Babraham – Mostly dating from the 13th century, but the nave
d aisle appear to have been modified and heightened in the late Middle Ages.

EFRESHMENTS:

ere are numerous opportunities in Sawston.
ie Three Tuns, Great Abington.
ie Peartree, Hildersham.
ie George Inn, Babraham.

Maps: OS Sheets Landranger 165; Pathfinder 1071.
In the wooded countryside around Stockgrove Park.
Start: At 921294, the Stockgrove Country Park car park.

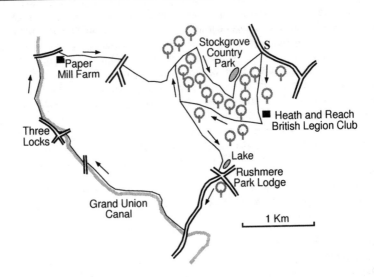

From the left-hand side of the car park, cross the little bridge beside the toilets and a
track to reach a sign for Baker's Wood. Follow the path uphill, ignoring a path on the
right, and turn right along a main track, keeping close to the fence on the left. Go
through a kissing gate and follow the yellow 'CR' signs along a path with barbed wire
fences on either side. Go through another kissing gate to reach the Heath and Reach
Royal British Legion Club. Just beyond the building, turn right through a metal gate
and walk ahead, following the CR waymarkers, and ignoring forks to the right. When
the track bends right, go ahead, crossing a stile. Now ignore all paths to the right,
descending steeply. Cross a bridge and climb up the other side of the hollow. At the
top of the hill, go straight across a track, then, when the wire fence on the right ends,
go straight ahead to reach the end of the wood.

138

The shorter walk now turns right along the Greensands Ridge Walk (GRW). Cross a stile and keep left of a pond, rejoining the longer walk after 200 yards, at a wooden marker post.

The longer walk turns left along the Greensands Ridge Walk, following the edge of the wood, with fine views on the right. At a fork, continue along the signed GRW to reach a road by Rushmere Park Lodge. Turn left to reach a crossroads. Go right for 5 yards, then left along the GRW into the wood. Now walk parallel to the road, first through the woods, then along the right-hand edge of a field. Go through a scrubby area to reach the road by a bridge. Turn left along the road to the **Grand Union Canal**. Just before the Canal bridge, turn right and follow the canal towpath for $^1/_2$ miles to reach Three Locks. Cross the first lock gate, following the Grand Union Canal Walk. Pass the Three Locks Inn (an excellent place for a pizza) and follow the towpath to the next bridge. Cross the bridge (leaving the canal) and go ahead, through the white gates. At Paper Mill Farm, go uphill with wooden railings on your left. Go over a stile and continue uphill to reach a gate by a house. Go through on to a road. Turn right for 20 yards, then left along a bridleway, following it past a fishing pond on the left and uphill to a wooden signpost, rejoining the GRW and the shorter route.

Follow the GRW uphill to a crossing track and turn right, as signed for **Stockgrove Country Park**. At the sewage works over on the right, take the left fork, following a well made path and keeping a fence on the left. Ignore paths to the right, descending to cross a small stream. Turn left to return to the car park, noting the site of the old boathouse by the lake on your left.

POINTS OF INTEREST:

Grand Union Canal – The canal runs from London to Birmingham and forms the backbone of the English canal system. Once a main thoroughfare for goods traffic, the canal is now used entirely for pleasure. Along the walk you can see boaters navigating the canal and working up a thirst at the locks.

Stockgrove Country Park – The park is jointly owned by Bedfordshire and Buckinghamshire County Councils. The vegetation of the Park and of its surrounding area is influenced by the underlying Greensand Rock. The oak trees and Scots pine thrive on the sandy soil and there is a mix of heather, gorse and broom in the cleared areas.

REFRESHMENTS:
The Three Locks Inn, Soulbury.
There is a tearoom at the Stockgrove Country Park Visitor Centre, open weekends throughout the year and daily (except Monday) from April to October.

Walks 73 & 74 **HARROLD AND ODELL COUNTRY PARK**   4m (6km)
or 8m (12km)

Maps: OS Sheets Landranger 153; Pathfinder 1001.
A fine walk through the picturesque Upper Ouse Valley.
Start: At 956566, the Visitor Centre at the Harrold and Odell
Country Park.

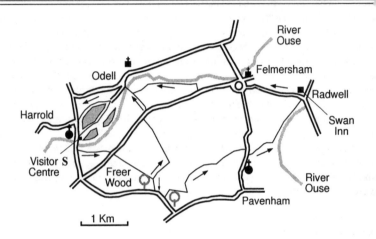

From the Visitor Centre, turn left to cross Harrold Bridge and immediately turn left
along a signed footpath into a field, heading towards St Nicholas' Church, visible on
the horizon. Cross a stile, and, at the crest of a hill, walk towards the farm building
ahead. Go over a stile and cross a road. Follow the yellow waymarkers over a stile
into a paddock, through a gate and over a stile on to a path. To the left of the path is
open farmland, while on the right is a ditch which is the old Chellington Hollow Way,
the route of the ancient road from Harrold to Pavenham. Cross a stile and continue
with Freer Wood on your right to reach a T-junction.

The shorter walk turns left here. Walk with a hedge on your right to enter a
thicket, then go straight ahead and, at the end of the trees, turn left, following the
yellow waymarkers. Walk with a hedge on your right, going around a clump of trees
and gently down through two fields to reach a road by Woodside House. Turn right
for 300 yards, then left along a signed bridleway, following it down to a river, rejoining
the longer route.

The longer walk turns right, following a track to a road. Turn left, then, after 300 yards, left again along a bridleway (after ignoring a signed footpath). Follow the blue circular walk signs, with Monks Wood on your right. Turn right at the end of the wood and walk downhill to a T-junction. Turn left along a track and go through two gates to reach a field with Hill Barn ahead. Go slightly left across the field, heading for a spinney. Bear left around the spinney and follow the track to a road. Turn right and, after 100 yards, go left over a stile on to a golf course. Follow the hedge, first to the left, then right to go down to a line of trees by the River Ouse. Turn left, following a black water pipe to a stile, ignoring a left fork. Cross the field beyond, following the posts to join a road at the Swan Inn. Turn left and walk into Felmersham. At the War Memorial, bear right down Memorial Lane and then turn left along Church End to reach **Felmersham Church**. Now turn right and, when you reach the river, turn left along Carlton Road. After about $\frac{1}{2}$ mile, turn right along a footpath, following the left edge of a field and crossing a stile to reach the river. Turn left along the riverbank. The path goes left, and then right over a stile. Now continue with a hedge on your left, crossing four more stiles to reach a cross path and turn right. The short walk is rejoined here.

Cross the bridge and bear right to Mill House. Turn left and follow Mill Lane up to the Bell Inn. Walk down Horsefair Lane and go through a gate into the **Harrold and Odell Country Park**. After 150 yards, turn right at the 'Footpath Only' sign and walk around the lake to return to the Visitor Centre.

POINTS OF INTEREST:

Felmersham Church – An unusually large 13th-century church with an imposing tower. The interior has many arches and columns and a 15th-century carved and coloured screen. There are only five church bells, but there is a legend that the sixth was thrown into the river after a quarrel between the monks of Odell and Felmersham. One of the village inns is called the Six Ringers.

Harrold and Odell Country Park – This 144 acre park was developed from former gravel workings and attracts many species of birds, especially wildfowl. The area is also rich in flora and fauna.

REFRESHMENTS:
The Swan Inn, Radwell.
The Bell Inn, Odell.
The Six Ringers, Felmersham.

WHIPSNADE AND STUDHAM   4m (7km)
or 9m (14km)

Maps: OS Sheets Landranger 166; Pathfinder 1095.
Two walks over the northern Chiltern Hills.
Start: At 009180, the Tree Cathedral car park, Whipsnade.

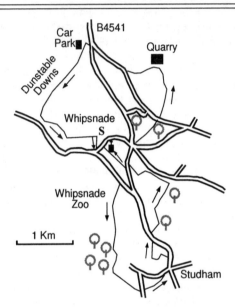

The shorter walk crosses Whipsnade Green and goes along the lane to the right of the
Chequers Inn. At a blockage in the lane, turn right along a bridleway, with the fence
of Whipsnade Zoo on your right. Go straight ahead where the Icknield Way turns
right, keeping to left side of several fields to reach Mason's Plantation. Bear left
along a signed bridleway into the wood. After 200 yards, turn right along a crossing
path to reach a T-junction. Turn left, and left again at the next junction, following a
signed footpath. At the edge of the wood, go slightly right to reach a stile. Cross and,
with a hedge on your left, continue through fields, crossing a stile and a small road to
reach The Old School at Studham Common. Cross the Common, bearing left along
the main path to reach a road. Turn right, and then left at the Red Lion, noting the
Clock War Memorial. Now, opposite the Bell Inn, go left along a footpath, following

t to a field. Turn left and follow the edge of the field around to a T-junction. Turn right and walk to a road. Turn left, and then go right over a stile just after the garage. Follow the path beyond through trees and open fields, and then past houses until you near a road. Now turn left and walk parallel to the road to reach a T-junction of paths. Turn left, then right along the road. After 150 yards, turn right along a footpath, following it across a field to a road. Turn left for 50 yards, then right over a stile. Follow the path beyond across two fields to reach a stile into the churchyard. Go through the churchyard to reach the Green, bearing slightly left to reach the start.

For the longer walk, after the churchyard, turn right on the road past Old Hunters Lodge to reach a crossroads. Go over and bear half-left along a signed footpath into Whipsnade Heath. Follow the path through the trees and then along the edge of a field. Cross a stile into another field and walk ahead to a road. Turn right for 60 yards, then go left over a stile and follow a path beside Greenend Farm. Go over a stile on to a track. Maintain direction to cross a cattle grid, and then follow the waymarkers along the right edge of the field. Go past a barn, on the left, and then turn left over a waymarked stile. Bear half-right uphill, passing a hedge corner, to reach another stile. Cross and walk ahead along Codlings Bank, passing through a wooded area to emerge on a track near a disused quarry. Turn left and follow the track uphill, bearing right when the track goes left, to continue uphill along the edge of a field. On reaching a building, follow the waymarkers left into the trees to reach a lane. Turn right and follow the lane to the B4541. Cross, with care, on to Dunstable Downs. Walking through a car park and a scrubby area, then turn left along the top of the scrub, following the waymarkers to a track and through a gate to a field. Cross this large field, with beautiful views to the right. Go through a gate, turn left after 30 yards, and then left again after another 30 yards. Now follow the waymarkers through a grassy area to reach a wide, tree-lined track. Continue past a house, then turn left over a stile and go along the right edge of a field. Go over a stile and continue past the **Tree Cathedral** to return to the start.

POINTS OF INTEREST:

Whipsnade Tree Cathedral – Founded in 1931 by Mr E.Blythe. It was inspired by Liverpool Cathedral and his experiences in the 1914-18 War. It is primarily a place of worship with different sections of the Cathedral formed by different types of trees.

REFRESHMENTS:
The Chequers Inn, Whipsnade Green.
The Red Lion, Studham.
The Bell Inn, Studham.

Maps: OS Sheets Landranger 153; Pathfinder 1002 and 1025.
In the eastern part of the Marston Vale Community Forest.
Start: At 107498, St Lawrence's Church, Willington.

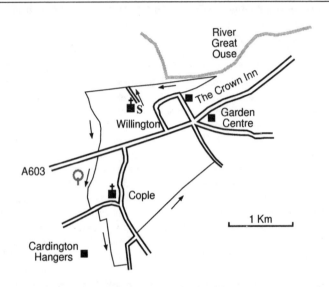

From **St Lawrence's Church, Willington**, walk along the road, passing the **Willington Dovecote,** on the right, and **King Henry's Stables** on the left. Keep straight ahead and, after crossing a stream, turn immediately left through metal barriers and follow the cycle track beyond. This track follows the old Bedford to Sandy railway line and then continues into the centre of Bedford. After $^1/_2$ mile, turn left along a signed bridleway to the A603 and Cople. Follow the grassy path over a stream, continuing to reach the busy A603. Turn right for 30 yards and then turn left, crossing the road with great care, to go along a bridleway, with a ditch on your left and **trees** on your right, following it to reach a road. Turn left to walk towards Cople. Just before the houses on the right, turn right along a bridleway, following it along the edge of Cople sports field. At a junction (which is 100 yards after a sharp left-hand bend), turn right along a track. Continue straight ahead, with **Cardington Hangers** clearly visible on the right, to reach a junction beside some broken down shacks. Turn left along a signed bridleway, following it to a lane. Turn left and follow the lane down to the main Northill Road. Go straight across and continue along the bridleway opposite, with a deep ditch on your right and open fields on your left. When the path joins a main track, turn right over a bridge and immediately left along a track. Go through double wooden gates on to a small road. Turn left to reach Willington Junction, with the Willington Garden Centre Cafe on your right. Cross the road, again with care, and go down Station Road, passing the Crown Inn on the right. Turn right by Willington Methodist Church, going along Chapel Lane. At the end of the road, take the concrete track to the right of No. 35. When the track ends, follow the edge of the field for 30 yards, and then turn left through a barrier. After 20 yards, turn left through a metal barrier. Willington Lock, a pleasant picnic site, is about 300 yards straight ahead. The track you are now following is the old Bedford to Sandy railway line again. Continue along it, enjoying the fine views of the River Ouse on the right, until, after more metal barriers, you reach a lane. Turn left to return to St Lawrence's Church.

POINTS OF INTEREST:

St Lawrence's Church, Willington – The church contains many monuments to the Goswicks who settled in Willington in the early 13th century. Sir John Goswick (died 1545) was Master of the Horse to Cardinal Wolsey.

Willington Dovecote – This quaint building originally had accommodation for over 1400 birds. Across the road are **King Henry's Stables**. Both these buildings are remnants of a 16th-century manor which was part of the barony of Bedford.

Cardington Hangers – The hangers were built to develop airships. In 1924, when the Government sanctioned the building of the airship *R101*, the hangers were extended to their present size (812ft long by 272ft wide by 186ft high). Unfortunately, in October 1930 the hydrogen-filled *R101* crashed at Beauvais in France killing all on board. Following a further disaster to the German *Hindenberg* airship, work was terminated at Cardington.

Trees – These are part of the Marston Vale Community Forest. The forest covers 60 square miles between the M1, Ampthill,Woburn and Bedford. At present woodland cover is only 3.6%, but the aim is to increase tree cover to around 30%.

REFRESHMENTS:
The Crown Inn, Willington.
Willington Garden Centre Cafe,Willington.

Walk 78   MARSTON THRIFT   5m (8km)

Maps: OS Sheets Landranger 153; Pathfinder 1024.

A woodland and ridge walk, overlooking the Bedfordshire valleys.

Start: At 955420, the village square, Cranfield.

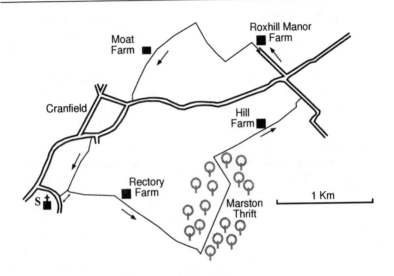

Walk down Court Road, passing the Swan Inn and St Peter and St Paul's Church, and noting the Gothic architecture of the village school, on your left. Turn left down Rectory Lane (signed for the Cemetery and Rectory Farm) and continue down the concreted track, with the cemetery on your left. At Rectory Farm, go straight ahead along a grassy track and through a gate signed for Thrift Way. Walk through several barriers, keeping close to the stream and small ponds on your right. Ahead on your right is one of the largest landfill sites in Europe. For many years clay has been extracted from the Marston Vale to produce bricks in the local brickworks. Now the pits are being reclaimed by filling them with waste and covering them with earth so that they can be re-used as agricultural land.

On arriving at the Thrift, go through a gap in the hedge, bear first right over a stream, and then immediately left along a grassy track, following it for about 300 yards to reach a sign for **Marston Thrift** (Wood and SSSI) on your left. Turn left over a plank bridge, go around a gate and walk through the wood. Go straight over a main cross track and, after another 200 yards, bear left, uphill, to reach the edge of the wood. Turn right and follow the blue bridleway signs, passing Hill Farm on your left. One of the two remaining brickworks can be seen on your right. Beyond the farm buildings the path goes sharp left, and then right. Go past a house, on your right, to reach a road. Turn left and, at the junction at the bottom of the hill, turn right and almost immediately left (signed for Roxhill Manor Farm). A few yards beyond the last outbuilding of the farm, turn left by a marker post and along a hardcore track. This recently diverted footpath is not shown on OS Maps. At the end of the hedge, turn right, keeping the hedge on your left. Ignore a path over a bridge on your left, and continue to a large gap in the hedge. Turn left through this gap and, after 100 yards, go through a gate. Walk ahead, with a ditch on your left, to reach Moat Farm. Go through an iron-railed gate, keeping the farm buildings on your left. Go ahead along a track and, as you approach a housing estate, go through the right-hand gate to cross a road. Walk down a path between houses, cross into Bedford Road and follow the sign for Salford and Woburn Sands. Just past Bowling Green Road, turn left down a track (Bowling Green Lane). Ignore two paths on your left, continuing ahead (signed for Marston Thrift via Rectory Lane) to where the track forks. Take the left-hand branch into a field, and walk ahead, with a hedge on your right, to reach the cemetery. Turn right, then right again at the T-junction to return to the village square in **Cranfield**.

POINTS OF INTEREST:

Marston Thrift – The woodland (chiefly of oak, ash, birch, maple and hazel) has been designated as a Site of Special Scientific Interest. The remainder of the area has been planted with conifers, pine and spruce. The whole area is being managed for wildlife: the lucky walker will see deer.

Cranfield – An ancient village dating from Saxon times. The pump in the village square was constructed in 1866 of ornate cast iron. The old rectory is Georgian and the church has many interesting features, including a blocked Norman doorway and a chancel roof heraldically adorned with shields of local families. Cranfield was once famous for its lace, but is now better known for its airfield. This was built in the late 1930s and was used in the war as a training school. It is now the location of Cranfield University.

REFRESHMENTS:
The Swan Inn, Cranfield.
The Carpenters Arms, Cranfield.

Walk 79   HOUGHTON HOUSE AND MAULDEN   5m (8km)

Maps: OS Sheets Landranger 153; Pathfinder 1048.

Visit the ruins of a house and enjoy good views from the Greensand Ridge.

Start: At 037392, the car park at Houghton House.

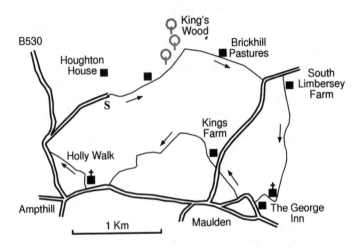

After visiting **Houghton House**, start the walk by returning towards the car park and going left along the signed Greensand Ridge Walk (GRW), just before the cottages. Follow the track past farm buildings and over a stile to reach King's Wood, an ancient woodland and now a local Nature Reserve. The GRW goes right here, but the walk continues ahead along the edge of the wood for 400 yards. Now turn right along a waymarked track, passing a barn to reach Brickhill Pastures (this is a slight diversion from the diagonal path shown on the OS map). Keep ahead through the farm and follow the concrete track to a road. Turn left for 300 yards, then go right along a path that crosses the corner of a field to reach South Limbersey Farm. Pass to the right of the farm and follow a track downhill. After crossing a stile, walk with a hedge on your left: Maulden can be seen ahead on the right. Cross another stile into Church Meadows, where the GRW joins from the left. Now follow the GRW straight ahead, keeping left at a clump of trees, and go through a kissing gate to reach **St Mary's Church, Maulden**.

Go up the steps and through the churchyard, with fine views of Maulden and beyond on your left. At the end of the churchyard, follow a metalled path which turns left down to George Street. The George Inn is a few yards to the left, but the route turns right, following the road until the GRW goes right, just before Cobbitts Road. Follow the path between fences, keeping straight ahead at a crossing track (follow the GRW sign) to reach a road. Cross, go over the stile opposite and cross a field to another stile. Cross, turn right and follow the hedge around to a stile, passing Kings Farm on the right. Cross the next field diagonally to reach a stile on to a farm track. After 300 yards, turn left over a stile, leaving the GRW. Follow the left edge of a field uphill, around to the right, to reach a stile. Cross and walk ahead to a stile into a small wooded area. Now cross a stile on to a farm track. Go left for 40 yards, then turn right across a field, heading for a gap in the opposite hedge. Go over the fence and follow a path to a stile. Cross and go downhill through trees to a lane. Turn left, and then right along a road. If you have time to visit **Ampthill** keep straight on, but the route turns right at St Andrew's Church, passing to the left of it. At a fork, bear left and, by Rectory Cottage, follow the sign for the aptly-named 'Holly Walk' which leads to the B530. Turn right, with care, for 200 yards, then right along a lane to return to the start.

POINTS OF INTEREST:

Houghton House – Built in 1615 in Jacobean style for the Countess of Pembroke. It passed to the Bruce family and finally to the Duke of Bedford who had it dismantled in 1794. John Bunyan is said to have used it as a model for his 'House Beautiful' in *The Pilgrim's Progress*.

St Mary's Church, Maulden – Largely rebuilt in 1859, but the base of the tower dates from the 15th century. The churchyard contains the family mausoleum of the Bruces of Houghton House and the remains of a medieval cross.

Ampthill – A historic town with many listed Georgian buildings and antique shops. St Andrew's Church is built of ironstone and dates mainly from the 15th century. It has an interesting memorial, to the north side of the altar, commemorating Richard Nichols. It records his achievements and also incorporates the Dutch cannonball that killed him in the Battle of Sole Bay in 1672.

REFRESHMENTS:
The George, Maulden.
There are several possibilities in Ampthill.

Walk 80   THE WOOTTON WALK   5m (8km)

Maps: OS Sheets Landranger 153; Pathfinder 1024 and 1025.

A walk through the fields above Wootton, with distant views.

Start: At 005451, the War Memorial, Wootton.

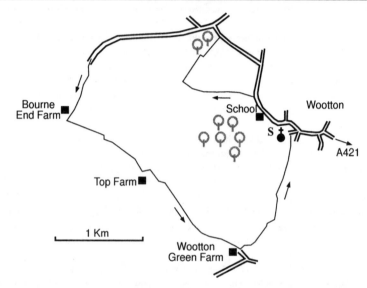

From the War Memorial walk up the main road, passing **St Mary's Church** and Wootton Upper School. About 150 yards after the school, where the road turns sharp right, go left up a signed track. Note that the 16th-century Chequers Inn is 300 yards further along the road. Follow the track, keeping the hedge on your left, to reach a stile. Cross and continue straight ahead across a field to reach a stile in the corner of the field that juts out. Cross and walk over a hill, with a hedge on your right, to reach a ditch. Go over two stiles to cross the ditch, and turn immediately right. Continue with the ditch on your right, crossing a stile to reach the corner of the field. Go slightly right through a gap in the hedge, over a plank bridge and then follow the path around to a road, keeping the barbed wire fence on your left. Turn left, then left again at the road junction to follow a road for 'Bourne End Only'.

After 70 yards, bear left along a tarmac minor road and continue for $1^1/_2$ miles enjoying views over the Bedfordshire fields. Go through a white gate at the sign 'No Through Road Bourne End Farm Only' to reach the farm. Go past the farm buildings to where the track ends, beside the Cellnet telephone aerial. Now turn left, away from the transmitter, to cross a field. There is no signpost, so aim for the tree you can see to the right of the telegraph pole ahead. In the dip, cross a ditch and continue straight ahead to reach the field corner. Note that if the field has been ploughed it is easier to walk around the right-hand edge. At the corner of the field, go right through a gap in the hedge and follow the left-hand hedge around the field and down into a dip. The path crosses a ditch and becomes a track: follow it up to Top Farm. Go left at the renovated farmhouse, and follow the track downhill, with good views of Marston Vale, Stewartby Lake and the remaining brickworks in the area. On reaching Wootton Green Farm, just past a barn on your left, turn left (signed for Wood Farm). After 80 yards, turn right over a stile (at a public footpath sign which is hidden behind the tree!). Keep to the right-hand edge of several fields, crossing four stiles. At the fourth stile, where you cross a ditch, head towards Wootton church spire, visible in the distance. However, the path follows the right-hand edge of the field around to a gap in the hedge. Go through the gap and walk with a hedge, on your left, and the recently planted tree enclosure, Celebration Copse, on your right. After crossing a stile, **Wootton House** can be seen on the left. Cross railings and go down a narrow alleyway, with houses on the right, to reach the entrance to Wootton House. Now turn right to return to the War Memorial.

POINTS OF INTEREST:

St Mary's Church, Wootton – The church dates from the early 14th century although there are records of a church on the site in 1166. The arches are the oldest visible part of the church, dating from 1310. Near the church there are several half-timbered cottages which form a part of old Wootton.

Wootton House – For many years this 17th-century mansion was the manor house of the Monoux family. George Monoux was the Lord Mayor of London in 1514. It is now used for the offices of a leading builder.

REFRESHMENTS:
The Chequers Inn, Hall End.
The Cock, Wootton.
The Fox and Duck, Wootton.

Walk 81   THE OUSE IN BEDFORD   5m (8km)

Maps: OS Sheets Landranger 153; Pathfinder 1025.

A walk along the banks of the River Ouse in Bedford.

Start: At 074494, the Visitor Centre in Priory Country Park.

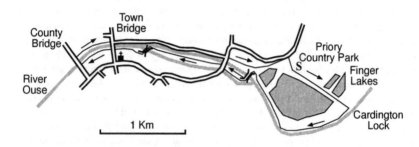

From the Visitor Centre in **Priory Country Park**, walk towards the lake and turn left, passing the finger lakes, on your left, with their bull and reed grasses. After rounding the bottom of the lake, turn left over a small bridge: a canoe slalom course can be seen on the right here. Continue ahead over another small bridge to reach **Cardington Lock**. Turn right and walk along the riverbank, as signed for the Riverside Walk. When the path becomes grassy, the Barns Hotel can be seen on the other side of the river. The hotel has been built around a 17th-century Manor House and a 13th-century tithe barn. Shortly after going over the humpbacked Fishponds Bridge, which crosses the entrance to the Bedford Marina, turn left over a wooden bridge into a meadow. Go half-right, heading back towards the river. Turn right and, at a path junction, go straight ahead under the new road bridge. After the path bears right, turn left to walk along the riverbank. In the summer small boats can be hired on Longholme Lake on the left. All the year round you will see rowing crews and lots of ducks, geese and swans on the river to your right.

Go past the attractive black and white timbered Bedford School boathouse and cross Boatslide Weir Bridge to reach a grassy area. Continue along the riverbank to reach a bandstand and, further on, Bedford Lock. After the path crosses another bridge over a large weir, turn right and walk over Abbey Bridge, Rink Island Bridge and Chethams Bridge to reach the Bedford Boat Club boathouse and the Moat Hotel. Go under the Town Bridge, and bear right to walk along the river, admiring the Victorian architecture of **Shire Hall** across the water.

Go under County Bridge and turn left up steps to a road. Turn left, cross the bridge and go immediately left down to the river again. Turn left under the bridge and walk back along the other side of the river, passing the Star Rowing Club boathouse, a car park where a market is held every Wednesday and Saturday, and Shire Hall. Cross the road by Town Bridge and note, on the side of the bridge, a plaque marking the site of the gaol in which John Bunyan was imprisoned in 1675. Walk along the pavement and then continue along a gravelled area beside the river. Go past a suspension footbridge and continue along the path by the river. Take the subway under the road (signed for the Leisure Centre), and continue ahead, with the Aspects Leisure complex on your left. At the end of the car park, turn right over a bridge, go through a wooden barrier and turn left along a gravel track. Follow this track around to the entrance of Priory Park. Turn right, passing the Priory Park Beefeater Restaurant to reach the lake. Turn left to return to the Visitor Centre.

POINTS OF INTEREST:

Priory Country Park – The Park is named after the Augustinian Priory established here in the 12th century. The Visitor Centre is run by the Bedfordshire and Cambridgeshire Wildlife Trust and is open every day except Saturdays. The lakes are used for sailing, canoeing and fishing.

Cardington Lock – This is the first of two locks seen on the walk. The locks were restored in the late 1970s, making it possible to cruise down the River Ouse from Bedford to the Wash and the North Sea.

Shire Hall – The Hall dates from 1879 and houses the County's administrative offices and the County Court. In 1961 the A6 Murderer, James Hanratty, was found guilty here and became one of the last men to be hanged in Britain, when he was executed at Bedford Prison in 1962.

REFRESHMENTS:

Priory Marina Restaurant and Bar, Priory Park.
There are numerous opportunities in Bedford.

Maps: OS Sheets Landranger 166; Pathfinder 1072 and 1095.

A walk along the upper reaches of the Lea Valley, with views of Luton Hoo.

Start: At 120203, the Someries Castle car park.

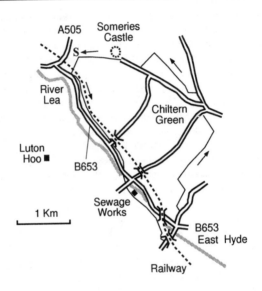

From the car park, go over a stile to the right of **Someries Castle** and bear half-right to reach a gate. Go through and keep to the right-hand edge of the field beyond, with **Luton Airport** on your left. Ignore the stile on the right, continuing downhill where the path goes into a track. When the track ends, continue straight ahead along a path to reach a house. Go under the railway bridge to reach a road (the B653). Turn left, with care, for 40 yards, then cross a stile on the left into a field. Walk parallel to the road to reach a gate. Go through and follow the marker posts, first straight ahead, then half-left up the hill. Continue to follow the posts up and across the field to reach a hedge by the railway cutting. Turn right and follow the edge of the field, with views of **Luton Hoo** over on your right. After crossing a road the path follows the course of the disused Luton, Dunstable and Welwyn Junction Railway which was opened in

1860 as part of the Great Northern Railway: sadly it was closed in 1965. The path descends steps to the B653 where the old railway bridge has been demolished. Cross the road, with care, go over a stile and up the bank to continue along the old railway track crossing the River Lea. Cross another road beside the Thames Water Sewage Treatment Plant, then, just before the path goes under the Luton to London main railway line, go right, up steps, to reach a marker post and continue along the left-hand side of a field to reach a road.

Turn left, go under the railway bridge and continue to a crossroads, going over the River Lea again. Go straight ahead, crossing the main road with care, and following Farrs Lane to reach a footpath on the left, at the end of the houses. Take this and, after 100 yards, turn right, uphill, along a footpath to reach a T-junction. Turn left and, after 200 yards, just past a clump of trees, turn right along a grassy path. Keep straight ahead at a marker post, with houses in the distance, to reach a paddock. Cross a stile maintaining direction to cross a stile out of the paddock on to a track. Turn left to reach a road. Go right and, after 75 yards, turn left towards Kings Walden. Keep straight ahead at Chiltern Green Farmhouse, and, after a further 200 yards, just after passing a cottage on the right, turn left along a bridleway. On reaching a field, turn right along its edge, following a footpath. Continue along a tree-lined path until it goes into an open field, with the airport radar and the Britannia aircraft hangers clearly visible. Now turn left and follow the edge of the field to reach a small road. Turn right and follow the road back to Someries Castle, noting again the view of Luton Hoo on your left.

POINTS OF INTEREST:

Someries Castle – A listed ancient monument. The gatehouse and chapel are the remains of a 15th-century Manor House and are an early example of brick building. The original bricks were used to build the nearby farmhouse when the castle was dismantled in about 1740. Joseph Conrad lived in the farmhouse for a time.

Luton Airport – This is the fourth busiest airport in Britain and the leading charter holiday flight airport. It is dominated by the tallest control tower in Britain which began operation in 1995.

Luton Hoo – This was originally built in the 13th century and occupied by the de Hoo family. The current building was erected in the 19th century. The beautiful park was landscaped by Capability Brown. The house is open to visitors in summer and has provided the setting for numerous films, including *Four Weddings and a Funeral*.

REFRESHMENTS:

None on this walk, but available in nearby Luton and Harpenden.

Walk 83　　　　　WREST PARK　　　　5m (9km)

Maps: OS Sheets Landranger 153 and 166; Pathfinder 1048.
A fine walk through the Wrest Park estate.
Start: At 083357, Silsoe Church.

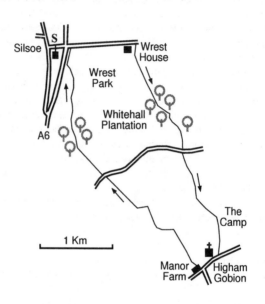

Walk past the church, through the gates of **Wrest Park** and down the drive to the house. At the end of all the buildings, turn right along a signed bridleway, still keeping on the concrete area. Go out of Wrest Park, between the brick gateposts by Cain Hill Lodge, and continue ahead along a track. The gardens of Wrest Park, with its multitude of statues, can be seen on the right. The track enters a wood by Whitehall Lodge: after 300 yards, just past a gate on the left, turn right along a path, following the blue Circular Route sign. Exit from the wood by crossing a plank bridge and then follow a barbed wire fence down to a road. Cross and go along the concrete track opposite. At the end of the concrete, bear left along a path, walking with a small hedge on your right. Keep to the left of a clump of trees and, after crossing a ditch, go through a gate into **The Camp**.

After looking around the earthworks, turn right by the gate where you entered the Camp and follow the fence to another gate. Continue ahead, with a hedge on your right, to reach a road. Turn right and walk through the hamlet of Higham Gobion, passing **St Margaret's Church**. Now, just beyond the road on the left to Hexton, turn right along a footpath through Manor Farm. Go left at the oil storage tank, and take the track to the left of a big open hay barn. After about 400 yards, pass a gate on your right and, after a further 200 yards, at a bend in the track, turn left along a field edge, keeping the hedge on your left. At a marker post, turn right across a field to reach a clearly visible wooden bridge. Go straight across the next field to a marker post. Turn left for 150 yards, and, at another marker post, turn right over a grassy bridge. Walk along the edge of the field beyond, with the hedge on your left, and then through trees to reach a track, following it to a road. Cross and go straight ahead over a plank bridge. At the end of the field beyond, go over a grassy bridge into a wood. The path emerges from the wood over a plank bridge on to a track: go ahead along the track, with views of Silsoe village ahead and Wrest Park House and grounds on your right. Follow the blue bridleway signs, ignoring the two yellow footpath signs to the left, to reach Wrest Park drive. Turn left to return to the start in Silsoe.

POINTS OF INTEREST:

Wrest Park – The estate is now owned by English Heritage and houses the Silsoe Institute for Agricultural Research. It is open at weekends and Bank Holidays from April to September. The French Renaissance style house was built in 1834 by the De Grey family near the site of an older house. The gardens are included in English Heritage's Register of Parks and Gardens of Special Historic Interest, because of their 17th- and 18th-century formal design which survived the later landscaping of Capability Brown.

The Camp – The earthworks of The Camp are medieval: the outer banks once enclosed a lake which may have been used as a fish farm to provide food for the manor of Higham Gobion. The large mound in the centre was probably a nesting island for ducks and swans.

St Margaret's Church, Higham Gobion – Built in the 14th century, but heavily restored in 1880. The year of the Spanish Armada is recorded on the beam above the chancel together with the initials HB - Sir Henry Butler, who was the Lord of the Manor at that time.

REFRESHMENTS:
The George Inn, Silsoe.
There are tearooms at Wrest Park House during the summer months.

Walk 84   **BARTON SPRINGS**   6m (9km

Maps: OS Sheets Landranger 166; Pathfinder 1048 and 1072.

A walk in the eastern Chilterns.

Start: At 086304, St Nicholas' Church, Barton-le-Clay.

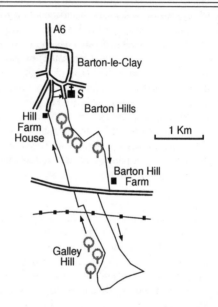

From **St Nicholas' Church, Barton-le-Clay**, walk up Church Lane to its end. Now
follow the signed footpath straight ahead, going through the kissing gate to the left of
the cemetery. The Barton Hills, soon to be climbed, can be seen on your left. Turn
right at the **Barton Hills National Nature Reserve** sign and, after a few yards, cross
the stream and turn left to follow it to its source at Barton Springs. On reaching the
Springs, note the water gushing out of the pipes in the hillside. Cross the stream and
go up a small rise on the left bank to reach a field. Bear right into a deep valley with
the hills ahead and on both sides. After 200 yards, take the left gully and climb very
steeply up the aptly named Windy Hollow to reach a stile at the top, by another Nature
Reserve sign. Cross and turn right along a stony track. On your right you can see
Barton Springs in the bottom of the dip. Keep straight ahead along the stony track to
reach a pair of white gates. Here, take the narrow footpath to the right of the gates to

each a road. Go right for 100 yards, then turn left along a bridleway. Go under the power lines and cross over a track, the **Icknield Way**. On your right is the South Bedfordshire Golf Course and then a large field. At the end of the field, turn right along a track (a signed bridleway).

Where the track turns sharp left, go straight ahead across a grassy sward, crossing the field to reach a barbed wire fence. Turn right and follow a track around the edge of the field, with the Galley and Warden Hills SSSI on your left. Now ignore a stile and missing gate on the left, and continue through a gate and up to the top of Galley Hill. From the summit (at 187m – 614feet) there are good views of the outskirts of Luton, and of the Bedfordshire countryside. Keep straight ahead, downhill, to go through a gate and cross the golf course beyond, following the footpath signs to reach a cross track and an Icknield Way notice board. Go straight across the track, following a path downhill and under the power lines. Cross a track and keep straight ahead, walking with a hedge on your right. Follow the field edge as it zigzags to a road. Turn left for 20 yards, and then turn right along a signed bridleway, following it through a row of stout wooden posts. After $^3/_4$ mile the track descends, with a disused quarry on the right, to meet a small road at Hill Farm House. Walk down the road to reach the iron gates of a playing field. The inns and shops of Barton are a few hundred yards further down the road. Turn right through the gates and cross the playing field to reach the tennis courts. Now take the narrow footpath to the right of the tennis courts to return to St Nicholas' Church.

POINTS OF INTEREST:

St Nicholas' Church, Barton-le-Clay – The church dates from the 13th century and has an unusually attractive chequerboard flint tower. It has a beautiful oak carved roof with angels and apostles, and some interesting wall brasses.

Barton Hills Nature Reserve – The Reserve is an area of outstanding beauty. The chalk grassland of the hills is of national importance for wildlife, particularly wildfowl and butterflies. The stream and woodland are the homes of many plants and animals which are scarce in the rest of Bedfordshire. The Barton Hills are believed to be Bunyan's 'Delectable Mountains' in *The Pilgrim's Progress*.

Icknield Way – This prehistoric way is claimed to be the oldest road in the country. It originated more than 4,000 years ago as a tribal route for trading all types of goods.

REFRESHMENTS:
The Royal Oak, Barton.
The Coach and Horses, Barton.

Walk 85 SUNDON HILLS AND SHARPENHOE CLAPPERS 6m (9km)

Maps: OS Sheets Landranger 166; Pathfinder 1048 and 1072.

Fine walking over prominent Bedfordshire Landmarks.

Start: At 048287, the Sundon Hills car park.

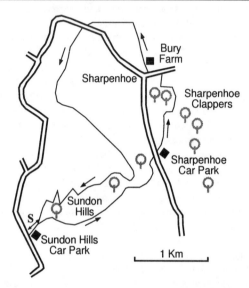

From the car park, go through a gate and keep to the top of the field, walking with a fence on your right. At the field corner, go through a kissing gate and turn right along a track. After 200 yards, turn right along a footpath signed for the Icknield Way and Bunyan Trail. At the next marker post, turn left, and then left again along a track. At the end of a few trees, turn right, following the Icknield Way. After turning left in the field corner, the path soon enters a wood. After a few yards in the wood, turn right and keep along the top of a ridge, still following the yellow waymarkers through the trees. When you reach a field, walk with the wood on your left, following the Bunyan Trail signs through a gate. Now, when the fence on the left goes left and left again, go right across the field to reach a road. Cross to a car park and continue straight ahead to **Sharpenhoe Clappers**.

Follow a tarmac track and bear right into a field. Go straight on at a waymarker post, and continue along a tree-lined path to reach a field with expansive views. Keep to the top path and enter a wood. Go immediately left up the bank to reach an obelisk commemorating the two Robertson brothers. Return down the bank and turn left along a well-marked footpath within the wood. Continue, with fine views through the trees on your right, gradually circling left, and ignoring the footpath going right. When the white houses of **Sharpenhoe** can be seen below, go right to reach a notice board and a yellow waymarker, and descend a path with steps. At the bottom of the hill, turn left in a field to reach a road. Turn left and, by the Lynmore Inn, turn right along a bridleway to Bury Farm. Go right, then left through the farmyard, leaving along a track with barns on your right. Shortly after a track joins from the left, turn left at a waymarker post with both blue bridleway and Bunyan Trail signs.

The path keeps close to the hedge, then crosses an open field, goes through a small gap in the hedge and across scrub land to reach a road. Cross and take the footpath opposite, following it along the edge of the field parallel to the road. After 100 yards the path bears left following the right edge of the field to reach a bridge. Cross the bridge and turn right to follow the edge of the field for $^1/_2$ mile, ignoring a path to the right over a bridge. Turn right when the path joins a track and, at a waymarker post, go straight ahead over a bridge and keep to the left of the field beyond. At the bottom of the woods, go over a stile and turn right along the bottom of the escarpment, keeping a fence on your right and ignoring all paths on the left going up into the woods. After a mile the path rises steeply up wooden steps: at the top of the steps turn left to reach a stile and a gate. Cross the stile on to Sundon Hills, bearing half-right and continuing to climb to return to the car park.

POINTS OF INTEREST:

Sharpenhoe Clappers – The land was donated to the National Trust in 1939 by W A Robertson in memory of his two brothers killed in the 1914-18 War. The beech-crowned hill is a designated ancient monument. The beech trees were planted between 1840 and 1850. It is believed that the hill was an Iron Age Fort and later a Medieval rabbit warren, the name Clappers deriving from the Norman French word *clapier* meaning a rabbit hole.

Sharpenhoe – The small hamlet below the Clappers. To the right of Bury Farm are the remnants of an old moat. This was the site of the Manor House, home of Thomas Norton, one of England's earliest playwrights. He was married to a daughter of Archbishop Cranmer.

REFRESHMENTS:
The Lynmore Inn, Sharpenhoe.

Walk 86   TOTTERNHOE KNOLLS   6m (9km)

Maps: OS Sheets Landranger 165; Pathfinder 1071.

Through villages of south Bedfordshire.

Start: At 987216, the Totternhoe Knolls Nature Reserve car park

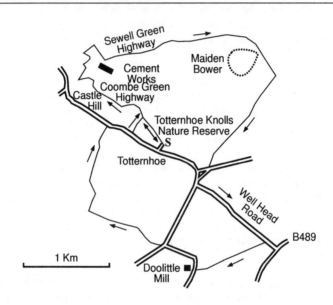

From the **Totternhoe Knolls Nature Reserve** Notice Board, in the car park, cross
the track and follow the public footpath through a barrier, with a paddock on your left
and a hedge on the right. Turn left along a track called the Coombe Green Highway.
There are fine views of Totternhoe and the south Bedfordshire countryside from the
escarpment. Keep to the track, following the blue CR signs, as it goes along the edge
of the earthworks of **Totternhoe Castle Hill**, on the left, and with a lime works on the
right. Eventually the track descends to some farm buildings: turn sharp right a few
yards before the buildings, following the yellow footpath sign. Go through a barrier
and follow the narrow path around to a small road, noting the lime kilns of the
Totternhoe Lime and Stone Company. Turn right along the road, which soon becomes
a dirt track. After 300 yards, turn right, uphill, following the blue bridleway sign. A

162

a gap in the hedge, just past the first large building on your right, turn left along a track called Sewell Green Highway. This track was once the main highway between the villages of Totternhoe and Sewell, and is part of a local network of ancient lanes that still remain. After almost a mile, by a blue waymarker post, a major track joins from the left: keep straight ahead, uphill, noting **Maiden Bower** up on the right.

Go straight ahead at a cross-tracks and continue, passing the Dunstable Town cricket ground, to the main road. Cross and go along Furlong Lane opposite, then turn left and, almost immediately, left again along Well Head Road. Note that the Old Farm Inn is a few yards down the main road. As you walk down the lane, Dunstable Downs is straight ahead and, in all probability, you will see gliders and parascenders in the skies above the Downs. Now, about 100 yards before reaching the main road (the B489), turn right through a gate on to a bridleway. Go through a gate and continue along the path to join a road beside the attractive Doolittle Mill. Turn right and follow Doolittle Lane around to a main road. Cross and take the bridleway opposite. On reaching some trees on your left, just before a lane goes left, turn right along a footpath. Go over a stile and turn half-left across a field to reach a waymarker post. Turn right along the edge of a field to reach a stile. Cross the stile and a bridge over a ditch, and go uphill to reach a main road. Turn right and, a few yards past Poplar Farm, turn left along a footpath, following it up a steep hill to reach the Coombe Green Highway again. Turn right for 100 yards and, as the track bends left, go straight ahead along a path to return to the start.

POINTS OF INTEREST:

Totternhoe Knolls Nature Reserve – The Reserve is on the site of a medieval quarrying area. The quarry produced Totternhoe Clunch, a hard form of chalk used in many local churches and also in Westminster Abbey and Windsor Castle. The chalk from the quarries seen on the walk is now used for cement production.

Totternhoe Castle Hill – The remains of the late 11th- or early 12th-century motte and bailey castle. It was known as the Castle of Eglemont (Eagle Mount).

Maiden Bower – The Bower was the site of an Iron Age fort (700BC to 43AD). Beneath are remains of a Neolithic causeway camp (from 4000BC to 2000BC). The fort was an enclosure formed by concentric circles of ditches, possibly used as a tribal trade and ceremonial centre.

REFRESHMENTS:
The Old Farm Inn, Totternhoe.
The Cross Keys, Totternhoe.

Walk 87   **BLOWS DOWN**   6m (9km)

Maps: OS Sheets Landranger 166; Pathfinder 1072 and 1095.

Although very close to Luton and Dunstable, this is a rural walk with good views.

Start: At 063198, the Village Green, Caddington.

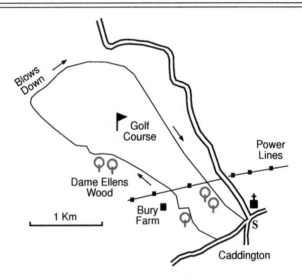

From the Green, walk down Dunstable Road, passing the Building Society Agency shop. Turn right along a public bridleway which follows a green lane opposite Mancroft Road. At a cross-track, go slightly left up a bank to reach a stile in the corner of a field. Follow the right-hand edge of the field beyond until a yellow sign points you to a stile near the telegraph poles, cutting off the corner of the field. Cross the stile and follow the path ahead across a field to reach the right-hand edge of a wood. Continue along the edge of the field, following the direction of the telegraph poles, until you reach a tarmac farm road. Turn right, and, after about 100 yards, at the end of Dame Ellen's Wood, turn left along the edge of the wood. Walk across a field to reach a hedge. Go through the first gap in the hedge and take the main path straight ahead, from which there are extensive views of Dunstable through the trees. Go over a stile on to **Blows Down**. Keep to the top of the Down to join a track which bears right to the top of the hill. The stone 'Private' signs indicate that the grazing land is private.

Keep to the left edge of the hill, looking over Dunstable, until the ground ahead goes steeply down at a hawthorn bush. Here, turn right along a path, maintaining height and passing a seat. Go through a gate and bear right along the top path through some trees, keeping close to the fence on your right. Pass to the right of the old chalk pits (there used to be a lime burning kiln here) to cross a stile into a field. Continue ahead, keeping on the top of the bank and going through a gate. There are fine views of Luton and the distant Warden Hills on your left. Just after a tree-lined gully comes in from the left, turn right along a signed footpath over a stile. The narrow path opens out into a field: continue along the right-hand edge of the field and, when it ends, go straight ahead with the hedge now on your left. At a gap in the hedge, go through on to a golf course, turning right and keeping to the right of the white waymarker posts. Turn left at the 12th tee and, still keeping the white waymarker posts on your left, go ahead to join a track. About 100 yards along the track, turn right along a signed footpath across the golf course, following the line of the yellow posts. On reaching the edge of the golf course, by another footpath sign, go straight ahead, following the left-hand edge of the field to reach a wood just beyond the power lines. Bear slightly left through a gap in the hedge and then continue with the wood on your right. The path goes into a track beside a caravan site on the right: continue along the lane, passing allotments on the right to return to **Caddington** and the village green.

POINTS OF INTEREST:

Blows Down – The Down is designated as a Site of Special Scientific Interest. It is part of the main scarp slope of the Chiltern Hills and its unimproved grassland contains a wealth of chalk-loving plants, with their associated butterflies. It also has a superb set of medieval terraces giving a step effect. These terraces were cut at a time of population expansion and land shortage in the early medieval period.

Caddington – The village once had a flourishing brickmaking industry with, at its peak, 15 brickworks. Now they are all gone and the Bedfordshire brickmaking industry is in the north of the county. However, some of the brick working sites are still visible in the area.

REFRESHMENTS:

The Chequers Inn, Caddington.
There is also an excellent fish and chip shop (SkyFrys) at Caddington Green.

Walk 88   STEVINGTON WINDMILL   6m (10km)

Maps: OS Sheets Landranger 153; Pathfinder 1001 and 1002.

A beautiful stretch of the River Ouse and a restored windmill.

Start: At 008528, Oakley Bridge.

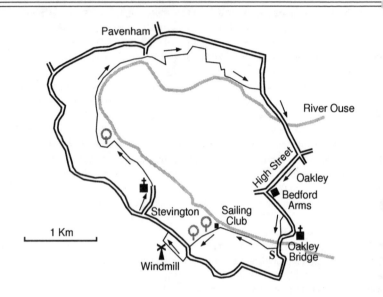

Parking is possible in the lay-bys by the bridge. From the humpback bridge, take the signed footpath over a stile, heading westwards along the left-hand bank of the river. After crossing a stile there is a good view of Stevington Windmill ahead. Cross another stile and, on reaching the Bedford Sailing Club compound, turn left along a track beside a tree-belt to reach a road. Go left and, after 80 yards, turn right along a bridleway. At a junction, turn right and continue to a farm. Turn left at the farm to visit **Stevington Windmill** (the key can be obtained from the Royal George Inn, in the village). To continue the walk, turn right to reach the road and turn left into **Stevington**. At the Village Cross, turn right down Church Road to reach **St Mary the Virgin's Church**. Pass to the right of the church and, after a few yards, bear left, following a waymarker and the wall. Note the Holy Well on your left here. Go through a kissing gate and continue straight ahead, crossing a stile to reach a waymarker post.

Go left over a stile and follow the right-hand side of the field beyond to reach a wood. Keep to the edge of the field, then cross two stiles and go through this small wood. Cross a wooden bridge, go over a stile and turn right along the edge of a field.

Go through a kissing gate, cross a stile and bear left, following the waymarker signs to the left of a thicket of trees. Now follow the path beside the river and, shortly after crossing a metal bridge, follow waymarkers to the left to reach higher ground. As you follow the hedge you look down on one of the most beautiful stretches of the River Ouse in Bedfordshire. Cross a stile and a small wooden bridge, and keep straight ahead, ignoring a stile on the left. The path goes over a stile into trees and then past a house to a reach gate on to Mill Lane. Turn right, following a waymarker through a gate (Landsdowne) to pass cottages and cross a stile. Follow the right-hand edge of the field beyond to reach a stile. Go right, over the stile, and follow the left-hand edge of the next field. At the end of this field, cross a stile on your left, and go diagonally right to reach another stile in the corner of the field, by the farm buildings. Cross the stile, following the Circular Route signs. The path goes over another stile and then bears right along a hedge-lined track. Follow the track left and right several times to reach the river again. Turn left beside the river to reach a road. Turn right and, at the next crossroads, turn right along the High Street. Just past the Bedford Arms, turn left and look for the waymarked path opposite Ruffs Furze. Go down this fenced path, following it as it curves around and crosses a field to meet the road at Oakley Bridge.

POINTS OF INTEREST:

Stevington Windmill – This is the only complete windmill left in Bedfordshire and the last in the country with common (or cloth) sails. It dates from the 17th century and was restored in 1951. It is a postmill, so called because all of the body of the mill can be turned to face the wind. The round house around the base was probably added during the 19th century.

Stevington – The Village Cross dates from the 14th century and is thought to be the cross at which Christian lost his burden in *The Pilgrim's Progress*.

St Mary the Virgin's Church, Stevington – The church has Saxon origins. On the north-eastern side of the church walls, in an arched recess, is the Holy Well, a natural spring which has never been known to freeze or run dry: It was formerly used for washing sheep!

REFRESHMENTS:

The Royal George, Stevington.
The Red Lion, Stevington.
The Bedford Arms, Oakley.

Walk 89   CLOPHILL   7m (11km)

Maps: OS Sheets Landranger 153; Pathfinder 1025 and 1048.
A walk through the fields of mid-Bedfordshire.
Start: At 093383, the Rising Sun Inn, Clophill.

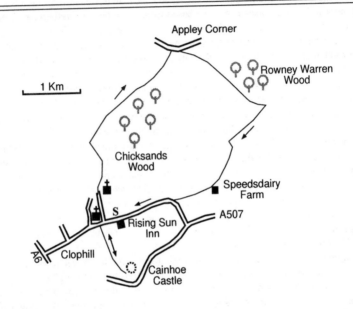

From the inn, walk back towards **Clophill** village, turning right after 100 yards up a track beside house No. 125, soon reaching the ruins of the **old Clophill Church**. Now, by a gate, about 100 yards past the old church, bear left along a grass track, following the green sign of the Greensand Ridge Walk (GRW). Cross two stiles and keep to the right edge of the fields to reach a plank bridge over a small stream. Turn right and follow the GRW signs for almost two miles, keeping Chicksands Wood on your right, but ignoring any paths into the wood. Finally, go over a plank bridge to reach a road at Appley Corner. Turn right and, after a few yards, bear right along a concrete track signed as a bridleway. After 1½ miles, at a footpath waymarker sign and an attractive timber and brick building, turn right and go through a farmyard, with a wooden barn on your right. Go over a concrete bridge, turn right for 100 yards and, at a waymarker post, turn left, uphill, to reach a barbed wire fence. Follow the fence to a gap in the corner by the water tower. The buildings on the left were once the Chicksands US Air Force Base, but are now used by the Ministry of Defence.

Go through the gap in the fence and follow the green footpath signs through the base. The route goes straight up the road, left at the end of the fence and, after 80 yards, right at a waymarker post. Leave the base through another gap in the fence into an open field. Take the clearly defined path down the field to reach a track by a large tree. Turn right towards Speedsdairy Farm. After passing to the left of the hay barns, bear right along a track which joins the old Shefford Road. Turn right and walk back to the Rising Sun, passing Clophill Fruit Farm, a good place to pick your own fruit.

A recommended extension to the walk visits **Cainhoe Castle**. Walk towards Clophill village for 200 yards, then turn left along a narrow path between houses Nos. 120 and 118a. Cross a stile into a paddock and, after crossing two bridges, go straight ahead, walking with a hedge on your right. At the end of the hedge you can see the tall mound of the castle ahead and slightly to the left. Turn left for 50 yards, then turn right to follow the field edge to a Clay Pit. Turn right and follow a track along the edge of the pit to reach a field. Turn left for 200 yards and go over a stile to enter the grounds of the castle. Return to Clophill by retracing your footsteps.

POINTS IF INTEREST:

Clophill – This is an attractive village with several 17th- and 18th-century cottages and Georgian houses in the High Street. Look out for the old village lockup and pound on the Village Green, next to the Flying Horse Inn and Restaurant.

Old Clophill Church – The church was built in the 14th century and was in regular use until 1845, when a new church was built in the centre of the village. For many years two services a year were held here, but after thieves stole the lead from the roof the church fell into disrepair.

Cainhoe Castle – The castle has a superb motte and bailey. Originally the Norman knight Nigel d'Albini fortified the sandy hilltop. There is a large, high motte with the original bailey to the west dug into an ancient quarry. Around this, two later baileys have been built, both well-fortified with earthen ramparts that would have taken timber stockades.

REFRESHMENTS:

The Rising Sun Inn, Clophill.
The Flying Horse, Clophill.

Walk 90　　**OLD WARDEN AND NORTHILL**　　7m (11km)

Maps: OS Sheets Landranger 153; Pathfinder 1025.

A walk through some picturesque villages in mid-Bedfordshire.

Start: At 138439, the Village Hall, Old Warden.

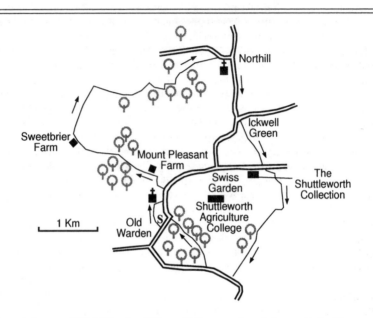

Turn right out of **Old Warden** Village Hall car park and, just past the Hare and Hounds Inn, turn right along a footpath. Go up wooden steps and keep to the right-hand edge of a field to its corner. Here, go straight ahead through a metal kissing gate and continue to reach the Abbey Church of St Leonard, noting the fine views of Old Warden Park and **Shuttleworth College** on your right. Go through another kissing gate and turn right along Church Lane to reach a main road. Turn left for 350 yards, then, at the Old Carpenters Workshop, turn left along the drive to Mount Pleasant Farm. Turn left at the gate to Mount Pleasant House and, after passing through the farmyard, continue along a stony track to Sweetbrier Farm. Just past the farm, bear right with the path to reach a signed bridleway along a tree-lined track. The Greensands Ridge Walk (GRW) soon joins from the left: go straight ahead, ignoring a footpath on the right, to reach the next bridleway waymarker post. Here, turn right, following the

GRW signs to reach a wood. Turn left for 25 yards, then turn right along a narrow path to reach a stile. Cross the field beyond, heading for a stile to the right of a hay barn. Cross this stile and another, then cross to the far left corner of a field. Cross a stile, bear right and walk to an open field. Keep to the right-hand edge of the field and, at the corner, turn left for 100 yards. Now go right along a path into a wood. Turn left at the T-junction and, after 100 yards, turn right over a plank bridge and stile. The narrow path emerges over a plank bridge on to a wide grassy track: turn right and follow the GRW signs to a stile by a pond. Cross and go ahead along a grassy path, heading for Northill Church, visible on the horizon, to reach a road. Turn right, then right again just past the church, to take the main road to Ickwell Green, passing the Crown Inn on your right. At the War Memorial, cross Caldecote Road and take the small road to the left of the Village Green. Keep straight ahead by Springwood House, going through a gate, and following the stony track to a road. (The Shuttleworth Collection Air Museum and the **Swiss Garden** are a few yards to the right.) Cross and follow the path opposite along the edge of the airfield, then follow the bridleway signs over two bridges to reach a pond. Go through a gate and across a field to reach the drive of Shuttleworth College. Turn right for 100 yards, then left along a signed bridleway into a field. Follow the right-hand edge and, when the ditch on your right bends, go slightly left to reach a blue CR sign. Continue ahead, ignoring a track to the right, to reach a road. Turn right and, just past a pretty thatched cottage, turn right along a signed footpath. Bear right at a fork and, 200 yards further on, as the track bends right, keep straight ahead, following the yellow CR sign. Go through wooden barriers and down a path into Old Warden. Turn left to return to the Village Hall.

POINTS OF INTEREST:

Old Warden – This is one of the most attractive villages in Bedfordshire. Many of the cottages, with their distinctive 'eye brow' thatched roofs, were built (in 'Swiss style') in the early 1800s.

Shuttleworth College – The College was set up by a Trust to commemorate Richard Shuttleworth, the heir to the estate, who died in action in 1940. The Trust manages the Air Museum and old planes can often be seen in the skies above the walk.

Swiss Garden – This 19th-century landscaped garden contains many interesting trees, shrubs, ponds and ornaments. It is open to the public between March and October.

REFRESHMENTS:

The Hare and Hounds Inn, Old Warden.
The Crown Inn, Northill.

Walk 91   **EVERTON**   7m (11km)

Maps: OS Sheets Landranger 153; Pathfinder 1002, 1003 and 1026.

An interesting walk through the countryside of east Bedfordshire.
Start: At 203513, St Mary's Church, Everton.

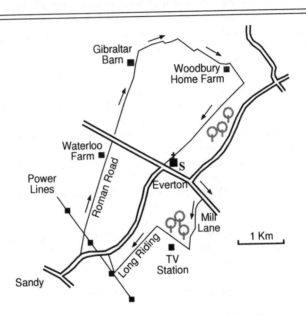

From **St Mary's Church, Everton**, walk to the centre of the village and turn left along Potton Road, by the Thornton Arms. Walk out of the village, passing the road to Gamlingay on the left. Now, just after Ashmore Farm, turn right along Mill Lane, a bridleway, following it towards the left side of the Sandy Heath television transmitter. The track becomes a narrow path as it enters a small wood. On reaching a concrete track, turn right and walk through the woods of the Everton estate, passing Oak Farm on the right. Shortly after the track emerges from the wood, at a blue CR sign, turn left along a bridleway known as Long Riding, walking with a wire fence on your right.

Go under the power lines and turn immediately right along a track to reach a road. Turn left and, after about ¼ mile, turn right along a 'No Through Road', soon turning right, at a metal gate, to follow the Greensand Ridge Walk (GRW). Follow the track as it gradually descends and passes under the power lines. Go through a wooden gate (as directed by the GRW sign), and follow a path along the right-hand side of a field. This part of the walk follows the old Sandy to Godmanchester Roman Road.

Cross a concrete track and continue to reach Waterloo Farm. Just past the farm, when the GRW turns right, go straight ahead along a signed bridleway. There are fine views of Everton Church on the hill side to the right from here. Cross a road and continue along the bridleway, with the disused Tempsford Airfield on your left, to reach a waymarker post. Go straight ahead, following the CR sign. A few yards beyond this post, **Gibraltar Barn** and some commemorative trees are just to the left of the track. About 300 yards beyond the barn, fork right along a stony track, following the blue CR sign. Just after the track bends sharp right, fork left and follow a good track for about a mile (as directed by the blue CR signs). At the bottom of a small hill, by a white gate leading to Woodbury Home Farm, turn left, following a grassy track as it bears right and climbs a hill to reach a concrete track by a white gate. After 200 yards, turn right over a stile, following the GRW sign. Cross the field to a kissing gate, go through and then walk straight ahead to reach a private tarmac road. Follow this road, with fine views over the Bedfordshire countryside on your right, passing Woodbury Hall (built in 1803) and Storey Farm (built in 1884) to reach the village of Everton and St Mary's Church.

POINTS OF INTEREST:

St Mary's Church, Everton – The church dates from the 12th century, although the distinctive tower and porch were built in the 14th century. A church has stood on this site for over 1000 years and is listed in the Domesday book. There is an ornate monument to Sir Humphrey Winch (died 1625), a Stuart judge whose pet aversion was witches.

Gibraltar Barn – The barn is on the edge of Tempsford Airfield which was built in 1941 and used as a base for Special Operation Agents in the 1939-45 War. The barn has been preserved and is a memorial to those men and women of all nationalities who flew to occupied countries and fought with the Resistance between 1942 and 1945. It was in this barn that they were given the equipment for their journeys.

REFRESHMENTS:
The Thornton Arms, Everton.

Walk 92　　　**SALFORD AND HULCOTE**　　　7m (11km)
Maps: OS Sheets Landranger 153; Pathfinder 1024 and 1047.
Fine walking in the Marston Vale Community Forest.
Start: At 936392, Salford Church.

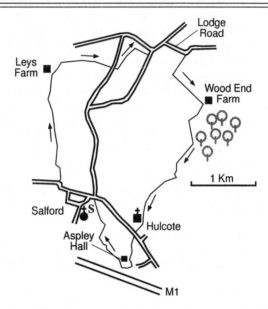

From the church in **Salford**, head south-westwards along Woburn Sands Road and, after 100 yards, turn right along Brittens Lane to reach a main road. Turn left and, just after Mill Lane, turn right through a gate, by a red-brick house, following a signed footpath. Go through another gate, turn left for 200 yards, then go through a gate and turn right along a hedge-lined path. At the corner of the field, by some trees, take the path through the thicket and continue uphill, walking with trees on your right. When the trees end, turn right for 30 yards, then go left at a waymarker post. Follow the left edge of a field, passing Leys Farm on the left, to reach the corner of the field. Go through a gap in the hedge and follow the waymarkers along the left edge of the field to reach a kissing gate on to a road. Cross and follow the signed footpath. After 400 yards, turn left at a waymarker post and follow the left edge of a field uphill, and then right along the top of the field. Just before the road, turn left along the field edge

174

to reach a road junction. Take the road to Cranfield, then turn right along Lodge Road. When the road bends left, go right over a stile following the signed footpath past a barn, on the right, and then downhill, with a ditch on the left. After 400 yards, turn left along the edge of a field. Turn right at a waymarker post by Wood End Farm, and, after going downhill, turn left by a large tree, following a **Marston Vale** bridleway sign.

In the corner of the field, go through a gap in the hedge and turn right, downhill, to enter a cultivated field. Turn left and follow a path along the left edge of the field. After rounding the bottom, turn left over a stile and plank bridge. Follow the left edge of the next field to a gate, cross a track, and a stile into another field (as signed by the yellow waymarkers). Cross the field to a stile near the telegraph wires and cross the paddock beyond to reach a stile to the left of the church in **Hulcote**. Cross and walk down the tree-lined avenue to a road. Cross the road to a stile. Cross and head for the opposite corner of the field. Cross a plank bridge and follow the right edge to cross another plank bridge. Now keep to the left of the tall conifer trees to approach a bungalow. Go to the right of a garden fence, over a stile and diagonally across a field to a lane. Turn right to reach Aspley Hall Farm. Just after going through a white gate, go over the stile ahead, by the footpath sign, and follow a concrete track along the right edge of a field. At the end of the track, turn right over a stile, follow the left edge of a field and, about 200 yards after the corner of the field, go left over a stile and follow the right edge of the next field around to a plank bridge. Cross the bridge and a stile into a paddock. Follow the telegraph wires to stile on to a road. Turn left, and left again along Woburn Sands Road to reach to the Swan Inn and the church.

POINTS OF INTEREST:

Salford – The village takes its name from the Saxon 'Seathford' meaning willow ford. St Mary's Church dates from 1200AD.

Hulcote – This was a medieval village based around Church Farm and Rookery Farm, but little is left now. St Nicholas' Church was rebuilt around 1590AD for the Lord of Hulcote Manor.

Marston Vale – Marston Vale is one of twelve Community Forests in England. Each area aims to create a rich mosaic of landscapes, incorporating woodlands, heaths, wetlands and farmland. Tree planting and the establishment of multi-purpose forest is intended to revive large areas of damaged and derelict land, producing timber and creating wildlife habitats.

REFRESHMENTS:
The Swan Inn, Salford.

Walk 93   **HOCKLIFFE**   7m (11km)

Maps: OS Sheets Landranger 165; Pathfinder 1071.

A walk through the fields around the village of Hockliffe.

Start: At 966270, the Village Green, Church End, Hockliffe.

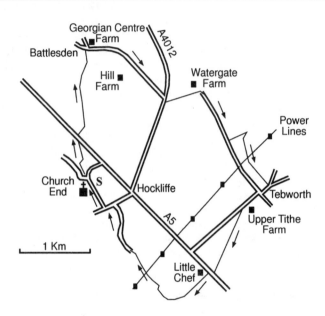

From the Village Green, walk along the road to the right of the church. Turn right to take the footpath opposite the church gate, following it along the right edge of a field to reach a stile in the corner. Cross and take the footpath half-left across the next field. Go down a small bank, cross the A5 (Watling Street) with great care, and go up a bank (by a bridleway sign) to reach a field. Follow the left edge to a metal gate, go through and follow the right edge of the field beyond, downhill to a gate. Cross a small bridge into a field and follow the left edge around to a gate. Go through and, still keeping to the left edge, continue to another gate on to a road in the hamlet of **Battlesden**. Turn right at the road junction, following a gated track, passing to the right of the Georgian Centre Farm. Keep straight ahead when the private road from Hill Farm joins from the right, to reach a road (the A4012).

Turn right for 50 yards, then cross, with care, and turn left along a signed bridleway, following it along the left edge of a field to reach a small gate in the corner. Follow the dirt track beyond and, in the corner of the field, go through a gate and cross a bridge over Clipstone Brook. Turn right and go uphill along a tarmac lane. About 50 yards after crossing another brook and passing a sturdy seat, take the first footpath on the left. Cross a field to a stile. Cross and go straight ahead to reach a double stile. Cross and turn right to follow the left hedge to a metal gate. Go through and immediately turn left though another metal gate. Go straight across the next field to an electricity pylon, and then follow the edge of the field to reach a double stile in the corner. Cross and turn right to follow the yellow footpath signs across fields, going through three gates to reach the village of Tebworth. Turn right through the village, keeping straight ahead along the main road at the Queen's Head Inn. On leaving the village, take the second footpath on the left after Upper Tithe Farm. Go half-right across a field to a waymarker post. Maintain direction across another field to reach a waymarker post by a small clump of trees. Go through the trees to a stile, cross and turn right. Cross another stile and bear right to a gate and the A5. Turn right for 50 yards (in the direction of the Little Chef), then cross, again with great care, and turn left along a bridleway. Follow the left edges of fields, uphill, going through two gates. At the top of the hill, in the field corner, turn right to reach a double stile. Cross and go straight down the hill, crossing two stiles to reach a footbridge over a stream by a farm. Walk to the left of the farmhouse, crossing several stiles to reach a tarmac lane. Turn right and follow the lane down to the main road at **Hockliffe**. Turn left for 100 yards, and then right along a small road to return to the Green at **Church End**.

POINTS OF INTEREST:

Battlesden – A small hamlet of four red-brick houses and two farms which were built for the Duke of Bedford in 1887.

Hockliffe – The village dates back to the 11th century. The name is derived from 'Hoga's cliff', the cliff referring to the hill on which the 14th-century church at Church End was built. The emergence of Watling Street as a main highway between London and North Wales led to the development of the village and at one time there were 14 inns and coaching houses.

Church End – This was probably the ancient centre of Hockliffe since the modern village has no church.

REFRESHMENTS:

The Queen's Head Inn, Tebworth.
The Little Chef Cafe, Hockliffe.

Walk 94　　**AMPTHILL PARK AND MILLBROOK**　　8m (12km)
Maps: OS Sheets Landranger 153; Pathfinder 1047 and 1048.
Along the Greensand Ridge, with fine views of Marston Vale.
Start: At 035382, the Market Square, Ampthill.

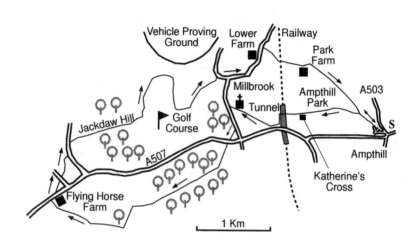

From the Market Square, go right along Bedford Street and, after 50 yards, turn left up Park Street. At the junction, take the second right up Park Hill. At the top, go straight ahead along a path signed for **Ampthill Park**, keeping the allotments on your right. Go through two gates to enter the Park by the Lodge. Go right, uphill, to reach a waymarker post for the Greensands Ridge Walk (GRW). Turn left and walk along the top of the escarpment, with fine views of Marston Vale. Just after passing **Katherine's Cross**, keep to the edge of the escarpment, crossing a track and following the GRW signs downhill to a stile. Cross the field beyond to another stile, cross and continue through a wood to a field. Turn left, following the path around the field, with wire fencing on your right to reach a track. Follow it to **St Michael's and All Angels' Church, Millbrook**, then bear left down to a road. Turn left for 300 yards, then, just after the cottages on your left, turn right along a footpath, following it up through a wood to reach the A507.

Cross, with care, and take the footpath opposite into a wood. At a clearing, turn right along a track and, after 40 yards, bear left, following the yellow CR signs. At the bottom of the hill, go ahead at a cross-tracks, then cross a stile into a young pine plantation and another stile into a mature wood. Bear right, following the CR sign, cross a stile into a field and turn right along its edge. At the field corner, turn left and go along the edge to reach a track. Turn right, and, after 200 yards, when the track turns left, go straight ahead, walking with a hedge on your right. Cross two bridges and follow the GRW signs over a stile on to the A507. Turn right and, just past Flying Horse Farm, cross, with care, and turn left through a gate, following the GRW half-right towards a clump of trees. Cross a lane and go uphill to a road. Turn left for 100 yards and, at Southview Farm, turn right along a track. Go straight ahead at a cross-tracks to reach Jackdaw Hill House. Go past the house, through the white gate by Poachers Lodge and follow the path through Jackdaw Hill Wood, with the escarpment on your left. After ignoring a path on the right, turn right, just past a pond, for 20 yards, and then go left. At the next corner, where you see the Vehicle Proving Ground ahead, turn right, with a golf course on your right. The path bears right, and then left at the bottom of a hill to reach a road. Go right to a junction. Go straight on towards Hougton Conquest. About 100 yards after passing Lower Farm, on your left, turn right along a footpath and cross a field to reach a bridge over the railway. About 20 yards past Park Farm, turn right over a stile and cross a field to another stile. Go straight ahead to re-enter Ampthill Park. Turn left along a path, going uphill with woods on your left. Now go straight ahead to the Lodge and retrace your steps to return to the Market Square.

POINTS OF INTEREST:

Ampthill Park – This was originally the deer park of Ampthill Castle. After the reign of King Henry VIII the castle fell into disrepair and eventually disappeared. The Park was landscaped in the 18th century by Capability Brown.

Katherine's Cross – Erected on the site of the castle to commemorate Katherine of Aragon who was imprisoned there by Henry VIII during her trial and divorce.

St Michael's and All Angels' Church, Millbrook – The church is built of local sandstone, the tower dating from the 14th century and the battlements from the 15th century. It is 360 feet above sea level and it is said that on a clear day The Wash can be seen from the top of the tower.

REFRESHMENTS:

The Chequers, Millbrook.
There are numerous opportunities in Ampthill.

Walk 95   **MELCHBOURNE**   8m (13km)

Maps: OS Sheets Landranger 153; Pathfinder 980.

An interesting walk through the villages of north Bedfordshire.

Start: At 028655, St Mary Magdalene's Church, Melchbourne.

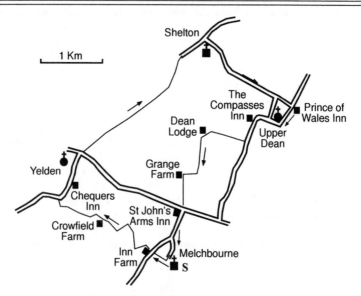

From the **church**, walk towards the village and, as the road bends right, turn left along a bridleway. After 30 yards, turn right along a narrow path between wire fences, following it to reach an open area. Go straight ahead, keeping close to the hedge on the right, to reach a road. Turn left and, almost immediately, right along a signed footpath, going to the right of Inn Farm. At the end of the farm buildings, turn right along a track, following it as it meanders through the fields. At the end of a clump of trees on the right, go straight ahead, when another track goes left, to reach Crowfield Farm. Go to the right of the buildings and then turn left behind a barn for 50 yards. When you are level with the green doors of the barn, turn right along a footpath across the field to reach a tree hedge. Turn left for 50 yards, and then turn right into a field. Follow the hedge on the right-hand side of the field to reach a concrete track at a Three Shires Way marker post. Turn right to reach a road, following it through **Yelden**,

180

passing the Chequers Inn and the motte and bailey castle on your right. Just before the speed limit de-restriction sign, go straight ahead along a concrete road (with a 'No Through Road' sign) following the Three Shires Way.

When the road goes sharp left to a farm, continue ahead, following the blue and white Three Shires Way signs to reach the village of Shelton. At the road junction just beyond the church, turn right along the road signed for Upper Dean. Follow this quiet lane for a mile, noting the disused windmill on the right. Now, when the main road bends right, go straight ahead along Shay Lane, crossing the ford: you can keep your feet dry by using the footpath on the right. At the junction by the Prince of Wales Inn, turn right. Walk through **Upper Dean**, passing Allhallows Church on the right, to reach a road junction. Go straight ahead along the road signed for Melchbourne. About 400 yards beyond the Three Compasses Inn, turn right along a tarmac track (a bridleway) to reach Dean Lodge. Go to the left of the houses and turn left along a track to reach Grange Farm. Follow the track to the left, through the farm buildings, with a pond on the left and the farmhouse on the right. Continue down the drive to reach a road and the St John's Arms Inn. Cross and go ahead along Knotting Road. Turn left along Park Road to reach Melchbourne and the church.

POINTS OF INTEREST:

Church of St Mary Magdalene, Melchbourne – The church is thought to have been built originally by the Knights Hospitallers. In 1264 the Manor at Melchbourne was granted to the Knights who built a preceptory, and held weekly markets and an annual fair. The Knights Hospitallers of St John (hence the name of the inn passed on the walks) were monks and soldiers who gave hospitality and protection to pilgrims.

Yelden – The village, the ancient seat of the Trailly family, is said to have been the scene of a great battle between the British and the Romans. As early as 1361, Trailly's castle was described as having fallen into decay. Today, the form of the moat and the mounds of the motte and bailey are all that remain on the Castle Hill.

Upper Dean – This was the home of Francis Dillingham, a rector of the parish, who was one of the 47 translators of the Authorised Version of the Bible. His memorial tablet is over the chancel in the church.

REFRESHMENTS:

The Chequers Inn, Yelden.
The Prince of Wales Inn, Upper Dean.
The Three Compasses Inn, Upper Dean.
St John's Arms Inn, Melchbourne.

Walk 96   THE OUSE AND IVEL RIVERS   8m (13km)

Maps: OS Sheets Landranger 153; Pathfinder 1002.

A river walk in mid-Bedfordshire.

Start: At 134516, Great Barford Church.

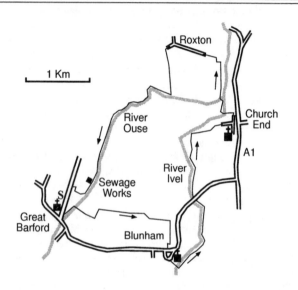

From All Saints' Church, walk towards **Great Barford Bridge** and turn left along the footpath opposite the Anchor Inn, following it down to the river. Turn left along the river and then turn right to cross the bridge by Great Barford Lock. Turn left and, after 40 yards, turn right over a stile. Walk to the far left corner of the field, cross a driveway and go straight ahead, walking with a hedge on your left. After 300 yards, by a disused barn, turn left along a track. After 400 yards, turn right at a waymarker post and, after a further 100 yards, follow the path to the right of a ditch, going along the edge of the field. At the field corner, cross a plank bridge and turn right along a track, following it as it bears left, with Blunham Church straight ahead on the horizon. About 100 yards after passing a white cottage on the left, turn right over a plank bridge and take the footpath straight ahead, following the yellow signs, to reach a road. Turn left and, at the church, turn right along Park Lane. Keep straight ahead when the road bends right, and, after a few yards, turn left to reach the River Ivel. Go ver the bridge and turn immediately left through a kissing gate. Now follow the iverbank to a road.

Cross and follow the footpath signed for Tempsford to reach a footbridge. Do not cross: instead, turn right, away from the river, and cross a plank bridge. Bear left o reach a stile and cross a field beyond, heading to the left of a dead tree. Cross a stile nd head for the far right-hand corner of the next field. Cross another stile and follow track down to reach Church End and **St Peter's Church**. Turn left along the old oad, by the Wheatsheaf Inn, and, just before reaching the main road (the A1), turn eft at a waymarker post signed for Roxton Lock. Go through the farmyard of Ouse arm and cross a bridge over the River Ivel. Turn immediately right along the riverbank. Jo through a kissing gate and turn left to reach a bridge over the River Ouse by Roxton Lock. Cross, turn right over a stile and follow the path along the bank of the River Ouse. At the end of a barbed wire fence, turn left, away from the river. Cross a stile on your right on to a track and turn left to reach Roxton. Take the first road on the eft, by a tree on a small green, following it around to pass a white cottage. Now, when the road bends right, go straight ahead along a footpath, following it to open fields and continuing along it to return to River Ouse. Turn right and follow the riverbank for $1^1/_2$ miles. The path then turns right, away from the river, heading for he local sewage works. Walk to the right of the works to reach a road. Turn left to return to Great Barford Church.

POINTS OF INTEREST:

Great Barford Bridge – The bridge is medieval, although extra building was carried out in the 19th century, and each of its 17 arches are different. It is a listed ancient monument. Locks were built on the River Ouse in the 17th century and Great Barford was then a minor port. In the late 1970s the locks were reopened and the river is once again navigable from Bedford to The Wash and the North Sea.

St Peter's Church, Tempsford – The church was built in the 14th century. A tablet by the altar commemorates a victory, in 921, by King Edward over the invading Danes who came up the Ouse in their longboats.

Blunham – The village has a strong Non-conformist tradition. A chapel was built in 1751 and several of the village folk were imprisoned in Bedford Prison along with John Bunyan.

REFRESHMENTS:

The Horseshoe Inn, Blunham.
The Wheatsheaf Inn, Tempsford.
The Anchor Inn, Great Barford.

Walk 97   ELSTOW   8m (13km)

Maps: OS Sheets Landranger 153; Pathfinder 1025.
Through the villages where John Bunyan lived and preached.
Start: At 048474, Moot Hall, Elstow.

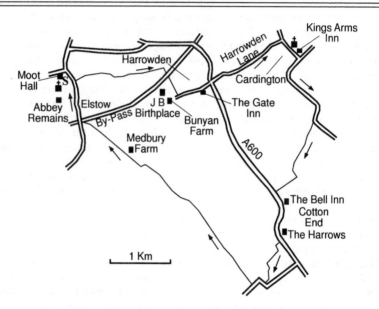

From **Moot Hall**, walk to the main road and turn right. Go past the Swan Inn, on the right, and, just before the road bridge, turn left along a cycle track, following it for about a mile, with a stream on your right. At a T-junction, turn right along a well-defined track. Go through an underpass below the new Bedford bypass to reach, after 150 yards, a path and notice, on the right, for the site of the cottage where **John Bunyan** was born. To reach the site, turn right and follow the edge of a field to a stile. Cross to a commemorative stone marking the birthplace. Return to the track and continue along it to Harrowden. At the junction by Bunyan Farm, turn left down a lane to the main road (the A600), passing the Gate Inn on the right. Cross, with care, and take Harrowden Lane towards Cardington. As you approach the village note the inscription 'SW1900' on the red-brick houses to the left. These are estate houses built by Samuel Whitbread, the founder of the famous brewery, who lived in Cardington.

Turn right at the main road, passing the cemetery on your right. Keep to the right of the Village Green and turn right along Southill Road, opposite the King's Arms. Follow the road out of the village, noting more estate houses on the left inscribed 'SW1894'. Cross a stream and a bridge over a disused railway, then, when the road goes sharp left, go straight ahead, following a signed footpath along the edge of a field. At the corner, go through a gate and then over a stile, keeping a ditch on your right. Cross a stile and the field beyond to reach a track. Cross a bridge and turn left through a gate by a telegraph pole, and go along the left edge of a field. Turn right in the corner and maintain direction over several stiles to reach a road (the A600). Turn left, and walk through the village of Cotton End. At the end of the village, cross the road, with care, and turn right along a footpath opposite house No.153. After 100 yards, turn left at a yellow footpath waymarker post. Follow similar Marston Vale waymarker posts along the edges of several fields to reach the backs of some houses and a road. Turn right, and, after 250 yards, just before the houses on the right, turn right along a bridleway. Follow this clearly defined track for about two miles, passing Medbury Farm, to reach houses on the outskirts of Elstow. Continue along Medbury Lane to reach the main road. Turn right, noting the ruins of the **Abbey and the Church of St Mary and St Helena** on the left. Turn left into Church End to return to Moot Hall.

POINTS OF INTEREST:

Moot Hall – This late 15th-century building now houses a museum of 16th- and 17th-century furniture and some John Bunyan memorabilia.

John Bunyan – The writer was born in Harrowden in 1628 and lived for many years in Elstow. From there he travelled the county preaching in barns and on village greens. When the Non-conformist movement was persecuted he was imprisoned in Bedford Jail where he wrote many books, including *The Pilgrim's Progress*.

The Abbey Church of St Mary and St Helena – This was originally the church of a Benedictine nunnery, founded in 1078 by Judith, a niece of William the Conqueror. After the Dissolution of the Monasteries, most of the abbey buildings were destroyed, leaving the present church with its detached 15th-century bell tower. John Bunyan was baptised at the church in 1628.

REFRESHMENTS:

King's Arms, Cardington.
The Bell, Cotton End.
The Harrows, Cotton End.
The Swan, Elstow.
The Gate, Harrowden.

Walk 98   RIVER OUSE AND BROMHAM MILL   10m (16km)

Maps: OS Sheets Landranger 153; Pathfinder 1025, 1002 and 1024.

Riverside and ridge walking, with views over Marston Vale.
Start: At 014477, the car park at Kempston Church End.

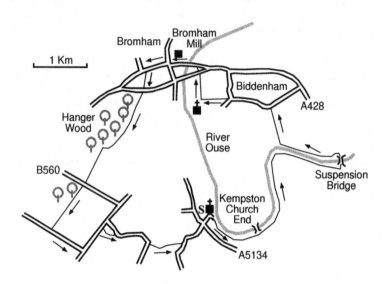

Turn left out of the car park and follow the road past All Saints' Church. When the road ends, continue along a footpath with glimpses of the River Ouse on the left. The path joins a lane: when this turns sharp right, go straight ahead along Church Walk and into Meadow View Road. Turn left along River View Way and go left at a fork to reach the river. Turn right over a stile, keeping the river on your left. Continue along the riverbank for $1^{1}/_{2}$ miles, at first on a path and then through open grassland. Cross the river at a suspension bridge, and head back (westwards) along the riverbank, following a tarmac path. Cross a stile and turn immediately right, walking ahead, with houses on your right initially, to reach a road at Biddenham. Turn left, passing the Three Tuns Inn on your left. Where the road forks, at the village sign, go straight ahead along a footpath (signed for the Village Pond) to the right of Dawn Cottage. Go

186

through three gates and continue ahead to reach the church. At the end of the churchyard, turn right along a track to reach the A428. Cross, with care, and continue to the old road. Turn left and, just after crossing the River Ouse, turn right into **Bromham Mill**. This is an ideal place for a picnic on the banks of the river and is an alternative start to the walk.

From the picnic area, follow the Bunyan Trail away from the river. Cross a bridge over a stream and turn left to follow the stream to Village Road. Turn left, and then right at the main road. The Swan Inn is 100 yards left at this junction. When the main road turns sharp right, turn left along Thistley Lane. Fork right following the Bedfordshire Circular Route sign. Cross the A428, with care, and bear right up to a gate. Go through and across an open field, heading for the left-hand corner of **Hanger Wood**. At the wood, walk firstly with it on your right, and then along a tree-lined path to reach an open field. Turn left, ignoring the Circular Route sign and keeping the trees on your left. Cross a road (the B560) and continue along the ridge to reach another road. Turn left, downhill, and, 400 yards after the road bends left, turn right along a footpath. Half-way along the field edge, turn left over a stile. Go diagonally right across the field beyond to a stile in the opposite corner. Cross on to a road and turn right, following it to the second sharp right-hand bend where a track goes off to the left. Here, head towards the lone tree in the field. If there is a crop, take the track to reach the end of the field and turn right along the edge. About 120 yards past the tree, cross a stile on to a track. Cross the track and go through a gate. Cross the open parkland beyond, bearing slightly right. Go through two gates to reach Green End Road and turn left to return to the start.

POINTS OF INTEREST:

Bromham Mill – The present mill building dates from the 18th century, but a watermill has probably occupied the site since the Domesday Survey of 1086. The Mill has been recently restored and includes an art gallery and exhibition area. Flour milling demonstrations take place on the last Sunday in the month during the Summer.

Hanger Wood – This ancient wood was referred to as far back as 1200. Lying along the Stagsden boundary, it has survived medieval woodland clearance which started from the centre of the parish. It is mainly oak and ash, but also has some rowan, hornbeam and aspen.

REFRESHMENTS:

The Swan, Bromham.
The Three Tuns, Biddenham.
There are tea-rooms at Bromham Mill during the Summer months.

Walk 99   WOBURN PARK AND HEATH   11m (17km)

Maps: OS Sheets Landranger 152,153 and 165; Pathfinder 1047.
Through the grounds of Woburn Abbey, returning over the Heath.
Start: At 951333, the car park opposite St Mary's Church, Woburn.

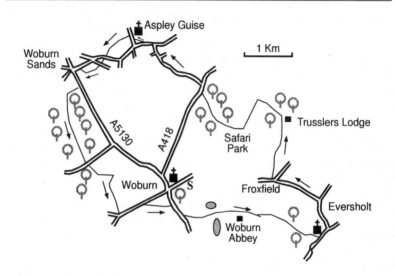

Turn left out of the car park and left again at the Market Square. After $^1/_2$ mile, turn left through a gate, at Ivy Lodge, signed for the Greensands Ridge Walk(GRW). On entering the **Park**, head for the left side of the **Abbey**, following the GRW signs. Go between two lakes, cross a road and go uphill to reach the Abbey car park. Go straight ahead along a track by the edge of the Abbey grounds and, where the road goes right, follow the GRW waymarker posts ahead to reach a gate. Go through the wood beyond, and down a field to reach a pair of stiles. Cross these and a bridge, and two more stiles, then bear left with the GRW to reach a stile and a road. Turn left through Eversholt. Turn left down Hills End to reach Froxfield and, immediately after crossing a cattle grid, turn right, following the yellow CR signs across the Park to reach a road at Trusslers Lodge. About 30 yards after crossing a cattle grid, go left along a track to reach the Safari Park. Go to the right of the entrance and turn left along the footpath opposite the quarantine building. Continue with the Safari Park on your left, then go over a ladder stile and through a wood to reach a road. Turn right and follow the road to the A418. Turn right for 100 yards, then cross, with care, and turn left along Horsepool Lane to reach Aspley Guise. Go through the village, passing the Wheatsheaf Inn on your right.

Turn left at the T-junction, then right along a footpath until it ends. Cross a road and, after 30 yards, go right through a small gate into a field. Keep to the left to reach a road. Go right and, opposite the church, turn left along a footpath, with a holly hedge on your right. Go through two gates on to a track, following it to a road. Cross and follow a narrow tarmac footpath, crossing a small road and then rejoining the main road. Go left to the centre of Woburn Sands, then turn left (as signed for Woburn). After 400 yards, turn right along a footpath and, after a few yards, bear right up an incline. About 20 yards past a gate on the right, go left, steeply uphill, along a narrow path (signed 'CR'). At the top, turn right along a track and, after 300 yards, go left over a stile. Cross a small bank to reach the corner of an enclosed area. Turn right, heading for the left of the tall trees ahead. At a waymarker post, just before the power lines, go ahead, with a hedge on your right. Cross a track and descend through a clearing, with trees on your left, to re-enter a wood. Bear right, following the CR sign to a stile at the bottom of the hill. Cross and walk to a road. Go left for 15 yards, then right along a path. Cross a track and then a stile into a field. Turn left to the field corner. Go straight ahead, crossing two stiles to reach farm buildings. Turn right along a track, ignoring footpaths on the right and left, to reach a road. Turn left and, opposite Maryland College, turn right through a gate and bear half left to another gate. Walk into the Avenue and, about 100 yards before the road, go left over two stiles and then right to the road. Turn left to return to the Market Square and turn right to the start.

POINTS OF INTEREST:

Deer Park – The Park covers 3000 acres. Walkers are sure to see many of the Park's one thousand deer.

Woburn Abbey – Built on the site of a Cistercian Monastery dating from 1145. It was given to the Earl of Bedford at the Dissolution in 1537 and has remained in the family ever since.

REFRESHMENTS:

The Wheatsheaf, Aspley Guise.
The Green Man, Eversholt.
There are numerous opportunities in Woburn.

Walk 100　　　　　TURVEY　　　　　11m (17km)

Maps: OS Sheets Landranger 153; Pathfinder 1001 and 1024.
A walk through the undulating farmlands of north Bedfordshire.
Start: At 942526, Turvey Church.

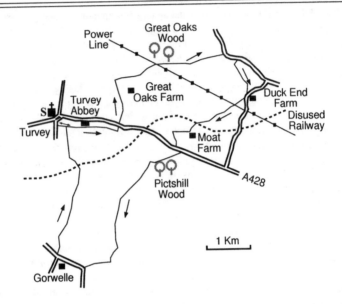

From the church, walk past the Three Cranes Inn to reach the main road. Go straight across and, after 70 yards, turn left down a track, signed as part of a Circular Walk. After crossing two stiles, bear slightly right, heading for the far corner of a field. Cross two more stiles to reach **Turvey Abbey Park**. Cross a drive and continue, with a stone wall on your left, to a stile. Cross and continue with a ditch on your left. Then, as you approach the road ahead, bear right to a stile. Cross and walk towards the silos clearly visible ahead. Cross a stile, turn left over a bridge and follow a hedge-lined path to the main road (the A428). Cross, with care, and follow the track opposite to Great Oaks Farm. After 500 yards, when the track goes right, go straight ahead, walking with a fence on your left. At the corner of the field, turn right, still with the hedge on your left. Go through two gates, then bear left to a gate in the far corner of the field. Now go straight ahead, passing Great Oaks Wood on your left.

At the end of the wood, a bridleway goes left. Do not take this: instead, go straight on for a further 200 yards and then turn left through a gap in the hedge. Walk with the hedge on your left for 400 yards, then, after going through a large gap, continue with the hedge on your right. Go through a gate, maintaining direction to cross a stile on to a road. Turn right for 300 yards, then go right over a stile by a post box. Cross a field to a stile, turn left for 20 yards, and then right for 30 yards. Now go left towards a telegraph pole, then continue ahead to reach a road. Turn right, then, 50 yards past Duck End Farm, turn right along a bridleway. When the trees on your right end, go ahead across an open field (as indicated by the waymarker). Go through a gate and, at the far corner of the enclosure, maintain direction across the field to cross a disused railway line, going through two gates. Follow the blue sign to pass Moat Farm, on your left. The path winds right to reach Pictshill Farm: go through a gate and turn left down the drive to the A428. Go left for 300 yards, then cross, again with care, to reach a signed bridleway on the right. In the field, double back for 20 yards and then go half-left, heading for the right-hand edge of Pictshill Wood. At the wood, bear right through two gates, go left for 30 yards and then right for 200 yards to reach a gap in a hedge. Turn left and go through two fields, with the hedge on your left, to reach a hedge. Turn right for 50 yards, then, at a waymarker, turn left along a track (signed for the CR). You will now follow these signs to Turvey. After a mile, at a facing hedge, turn right and keep the hedge on your left to reach a road. Turn right to reach a junction at Gorwelle. Turn right and, when the road goes left, go ahead along a path, following it for a mile. Cross a ditch at the bottom of a dip, go left for a few yards and then right, uphill, to a driveway. Go straight ahead, crossing the disused railway line again. Now, just before a cottage on the left, turn right along a footpath. Cross a stile, and bear left to cross two more stiles. Continue to reach a road and turn right to return to **Turvey Church**.

POINTS OF INTEREST:

Turvey Abbey Park – Before 1783, when the Park was enclosed, it was part of Turvey's open, common fields – communally cultivated arable fields. The ridge and furrow remains can be seen along the walk.

All Saints' Church, Turvey – The church is one of the finest in Bedfordshire. The oldest parts are Saxon, including the massive oak doors overlaid with rich ornamental ironwork.

REFRESHMENTS:

The Three Cranes, Turvey.
The Three Fyshes, Turvey. This inn, by the river, dates from 1622.